THE BALANCE OF
SITUATED ACTION AND FORMAL INSTRUCTION
FOR LEARNING CONDITIONAL REASONING

Copyright © 1995 Jelke van der Pal

Cover design: Dick Rutgers bNO, Groningen
Print: CopyPrint 2000, Enschede

CIP-DATA KONINKLIJKE BIBLIOTHEEK, DEN HAAG

Pal, Jelke van der

The balance of situated action and formal instruction for learning conditional reasoning /
Jelke van der Pal. - [S.l. : s..n.]. - Ill.
Thesis Universiteit Twente Enschede - With ref.
ISBN 90-9008710-9
Subjects headings: cognition / computer-assisted instruction.

THE BALANCE OF SITUATED ACTION AND FORMAL INSTRUCTION FOR LEARNING CONDITIONAL REASONING

PROEFSCHRIFT

ter verkrijging van de graad van doctor
aan de Universiteit Twente, op gezag van
de rector magnificus, prof. dr.Th. J. A. Popma
volgens het besluit van het College van Promoties
in het openbaar te verdedigen op
donderdag 12 oktober 1995 te 13.15 uur.

door

Jelke van der Pal
geboren op 26 september 1963 te Leeuwarden

Dit proefschrift is goedgekeurd door de promotor:

Prof. dr. S. Dijkstra

Referent:

Dr. H.P.M. Krammer

Deprived of thought, the word is dead.
However, thought that is not embodied
in the word remains a Stygian shadow.

Lev Vygotsky
Thinking and Speech, 1934

But, although they [i.e., the most general
and greatest concepts] may not have
meaning, they do make sense, and it is
very sensible to awaken this sense from
time to time.

Robert Musil
Der Mann ohne Eigenschaften
(first book), 1924
(translation by Jelke van der Pal)

Contents

Acknowledgements		xi
Preface		xiii
1	**Introduction and Overview**	1
1.1	A Theoretical Load on Tarski's World	1
1.2	Research on Logic Instruction	2

PART I Theory

2	**The Psychology of Situated Action**	7
2.1	What is Wrong with Cognitivism?	7
2.2	Situated Action	11
	Situated Action versus Cognitivism	12
	Vygotsky's Dynamic Bridge from Nature to Culture	14
	Formality in Situated Action: The Developmental Situativity Theory	19
2.3	Instructional Design and the Developmental Situativity Theory	21

3	**The Psychology of Deductive Reasoning**	25
3.1	The Questions of Competence, Bias, and Content	25
3.2	Conditional Reasoning	26
	The Wason Selection Task	26
	Theories of Reasoning	29
3.3	Learning to Reason: A Pragmatic View	32

PART II Introduction in Logic

4	**Tarski's World: Computer-based Instruction in First-order Predicate Logic**	39
4.1	The Importance of Logic Instruction	39
4.2	The Look of Tarski's World	40
4.3	The Significance of Tarski's World	46
	Situativity-in-Domain in Tarski's World	48
4.4	Tarski's World in an Experimental Environment	49
	Experimental Impairment of Tarski's World	50
	Instructional Design for the Material Conditional	52
	Implementation of the Research Version of Tarski's World	56

PART III Research with Tarski's World

5	**Situativity versus Formality in Logic Instruction, Part 1**	63
5.1	Introduction	63
5.2	The Pilot Experiment	64
	Method	64
	Results	66
	Discussion	67
5.3	An Experiment	71
	Method	71
	Results	72
	Discussion	73
5.4	General Discussion	75
6	**The Role of Explanation in Logic Instruction**	79
6.1	Introduction	79
6.2	Formal Explanation in Text and Game	80
	Method	81
	Results	83
	Discussion	86

7	Situativity versus Formality in Logic Instruction, Part 2	91
7.1	Introduction	91
7.2	Method	94
7.3	Results	95
7.4	Discussion	98

PART IV Discussion

8	General Discussion and epilogue	103
8.1	Conclusion and Value of this Study	103
8.2	Theoretical Implications	105
8.3	Research Implications	108
8.4	Instructional Implications	111

References	117
Samenvatting (Dutch Summary)	127
Appendix A	131
A.1 Instructional Material for the Experiment of Chapter 7	131
A.2 Instructional Material for the Pilot Study of Chapter 5: Major Differences from the Material of Chapter 7	145
A.3 Instructional Material for the Experiment of Chapter 5: Major Differences from the Material of Chapter 7	147
A.4 Instructional Material for the Experiment of Chapter 6: Major Differences from the Material of Chapter 7	148

Acknowledgements

I am indebted to many persons for several reasons. Their support and criticisms have been crucial for the research and this book. I especially would like to thank:

Sanne Dijkstra for his instant recognition of the significance of Tarski's World and for the intellectual freedom and support I have experienced in the four years I have served at the department of Instructional Technology;

Hein Krammer in particular for the lifely discussions in the important early part of the project;

Jules Pieters, Jeroen van Merriënboer, Jan Gerrit Schuurman and Ard Lazonder for (p)reviewing various manuscripts underlying this thesis;

Jon Barwise (Indiana University) and John Etchemendy (Stanford University) for making available the source code of Tarski's World 3.1 in order to meet the experimental requirements for this thesis;

Jacob Sikken for his part in programming the research version of Tarski's World;

Gerard Baars and Ellen Peters for their assistance during the experiments;

Dick Rutgers for designing the cover and for his layout suggestions;

Ard Lazonder again, for being a great silly room-mate, and for the many serious discussions too;

The colleagues of the faculty of Education with whom I had a nice time and the secretaries Pauline Teppich and Thyra Kamphuis-Kuijpers who have been helpful and provided a pleasant atmosphere;

Last but not least, Afineke de Vries for her linguistic corrections on this thesis and for being with me.

Preface

You just won in a quiz. Unfortunately, the prize is behind one of three doors. You have to open a door to collect your prize or to get nothing! You choose one door, but just before opening it, the quizmaster —who obviously knows— intervenes by opening one of the other doors which has no prize behind it. He asks you whether you stick to your choice or whether you switch to the other door. What is your decision?

This three doors problem has held many readers, among which many professors and university level engineers, of a Dutch newspaper article on Bayesian statistics in its grip for several weeks. Intuitively, most people respond that it doesn't matter as the quizmaster created a new situation: The prize is now behind one of *two* doors: a chance of 1/2 for each alternative. You may as well open the door of your initial choice. However, those who are skilled in Bayesian statistics do not carelessly dispose of the initial information. Using Bayes theorem correctly, they will find a chance of 1/3 when you do not switch and a chance of 2/3 when you do switch. Others construct a non-mathematical external representation, e.g., a 3x2 table: three rows for the first choice (selecting a door: right, wrong, wrong) and two columns for the second choice (switching, no switching). The cells of the table inform about the combination of the two choices: prize or no prize. The table confirms the Bayesian outcome.

Many people did not trust any external representation leading to other conclusions than the intuitive one. Some of those tried to find comfort in the ultimate evidence: the experiment. To their astonishment they found themselves supporting Bayes theorem, which lead them to accept, but not to understand the wrongness of their choice. One professor still hoped that there was an error in his simulation program. In contrast, some mathematical experts fail (or pretend to fail) to understand why the intuitions of other, intelligent persons are so different.

The three doors problem is a problem of intuition, but one that needs an intuition that may have been developed only after considerable experience with 'formal' methods (including non-mathematical external representations). The importance of and differences between intuitive and formal thinking, and how to bridge these two via instruction is the central topic of this thesis. Problems like the three doors problem are interesting as a research paradigm for the study of thinking and learning. In this thesis, I will use another selection problem that needs a counterintuitive solution: the abstract Wason's selection task. To solve this problem, one has to apply an elementary rule in formal logic. This task is even more intriguing than the three doors problem because generally most people fail to succeed, *do* understand the correct solution when explained, but fail again on an equivalent selection task. Formal logic is not merely the instructional domain in this thesis. In fact it plays a triple role. By describing these roles, I hope the reader will get an impression of the content of this thesis.

In its first role, formal logic will be the matter to be instructed to undergraduate students with a computer program that has been promised by the developers to constitute a thorough semantical basis for the study of logic. It is the emphasis on semantics that has lead me to the psychological field of conditional reasoning.

The abundant if-then expressions in everyday life do not follow the formal meaning of their logical pendant, the material conditional. Now, this should not be really surprising as logicians have deliberately stripped off the everyday connotations of conditional expressions in order to be able to have an unambigious and rigorous semantics for the connective. Through such definitions, logicians were able to construct a calculus of predicates in which operations are purely syntactic. The meaning of the resulting expression had to be reconstructed later on. The purpose of this enterprise was to construct a solid basis for mathematics, but logicians, and many cognitive psychologists too, believed that the human mind, although liable to error, operated syntactically and consistent to this mathematical logic and its accompanying set theory. Therefore, many psychologists in the sixties and early seventies were surprised by the accumulating empirical data against syntactic processing of information. Logic as the input of the debate on the nature of reasoning forms its second role in this thesis.

Much more surprising was the fact that instruction in the material conditional appeared to have no effect on problems that clearly need the application of the material conditional to solve it. This even holds when instruction was very concrete with test problems much alike the instruction tasks. Recently however, some learning effects have been established, but from an instructional point of view the effects are weak or inefficient. Three decenniums of research on conditional reasoning has shown us that it is only possible to facilitate logical conditional reasoning in very restricted ways. The computer-assisted instruction I referred to, which is Tarski's World written by Jon Barwise and John Etchemendy, is completely different from other logic instruction and due to its focus on semantics I credited it for the ability to establish a strong understanding of the material conditional. Such understanding would be strong enough to apply the material conditional in situations other than those in Tarski's World, e.g., the task that has been the primal research paradigm in conditional reasoning studies: the Wason selection task. This thesis reports about an unprecedented learning effect, although it was far less easy to establish it than I expected at the start of the project by the end of 1990.

Logic plays its third role when it comes to explaining the success of Tarski's World. The prevalent psychological and instructional paradigm is cognitivism. The core idea of cognitivism is that information processing is symbolic, which means that it is syntactic and that meaning of symbols are somehow reconstructed. In other words, human knowledge is subject to some kind of formal logic. Research on conditional reasoning and research on categorization in the 70s has made a strong claim undefendable. Standard logic (first-order predicate logic) and its set theory does not provide us with an adequate language to describe human knowledge and processing of information. Most cognitivists nowadays hold a weaker position, but even this has been criticised upon in the eighties. I follow these critics and place myself into an anti-cognitivist position. Formal logic of any kind cannot be used as a basis for (representational) cognitive psychological theories.

It is ironical that in order to understand how logical conditional reasoning can be learned efficiently, one has to reject the use of formal logic for constraining and determining theoretical assumptions on cognition. Exit formal logic in psychology? Certainly not. Where cognition in itself does not necessarily follow a logic or can be simulated by it, the processes underlying cognition may be described by some logic system, as for instance in connectionism.

Another ironic point is that where formal logic plays such eminent and difficult roles in nearly all parts of this thesis, the main actors are learning and instruction. It is my intention to show that these actors can play better roles than they did under a cognitivistic director.

1

Introduction and Overview

1.1 A Theoretical Load on Tarski's World

In this thesis several experiments are reported that make use of Tarski's World, a computer-assisted instruction for an introduction in formal logic. This program, written by Barwise and Etchemendy which has been released since 1987, is more than just another logic instruction as it embodies an unconventional view on logic instruction, and it was way ahead of its time in instructional technology. Even nowadays, after eight years, the program looks fresh and invites logicians, learning theorists, and instructional technologists to wonder about what makes this program attractive and significant.

As with an interesting piece of art, Tarski's World can be interpreted in several ways. It was Greeno's (1990) view that put Tarski's World in a situated cognition realm. Situated cognition as it was debated within the field of instructional technology in the late eighties provided a new escape route from formal education. Within purely formal education, knowledge is taken to be a static set of abstract concepts and procedures which are assumed to be taught by exposing their formal representations to the students in some way or another. Although education based on situated cognition may be refreshing in itself (with its emphasis on authentic experiences), the enterprise was also annoying because it is yet another repetition of history in which some formal education is counterbalanced with some naturalistic education. The purpose of dialectics is to reach a synthesis, without that intention dialectics is senseless. By pointing to Tarski's World, Greeno illustrated that the formalist - naturalist debate is not really important on the instructional level: Tarski's World has very formal aspects and yet it elicits situated action from students. This recognition has lead to the formulation of the research question that will be introduced in the next section.

A situated action (including situated cognition) theory cannot simply be referred to as the theoretical background of a series of experiments. There is much controversy about situated action and there are many positions that can be taken. For that reason, I will explicate my position about situated action in chapter 2. In that chapter, situated action will be compared to cognitivism, which is a natural thing to do because situated action theory has the potential of a Kuhnian paradigm. It is expected that situated action theory will take over the leading position of cognitivism in cognitive science. Some theorists have claimed situated action theory to be the synthesis of behaviorism and cognitivism (Greeno & Moore, 1993). For the purpose of this thesis, situated action will be worked out by relating it to connectionism and Vygotsky's developmental psychology.

1.2 Research on Logic Instruction

One of the purposes of Tarski's World is that undergraduate students will gain insight in semantical aspects of formal logic. This implies that students are expected to be able to use the logical definition of if - then rules (the material conditional). This is a rather audacious assertion because reasoning psychologists have been puzzled for nearly three decenniums by conditional reasoning and the inability of people to learn to use the modus tollens in the Wason selection task. It will be clear that the first question in this thesis is: Does Tarski's World instruction facilitate logical reasoning in the Wason selection task? Because the present study is continuating the research on conditional reasoning, this domain will be reviewed in chapter 3.

A positive answer to the research question of the previous paragraph would be important as no short-term instruction has ever lead to far transfer of logical conditional reasoning. The second and more important question is: What are the design principles behind Tarski's World which facilitate this effect? I believe such principles are subject to general learning processes that go beyond the scope of behavioristic or cognitivistic learning theories which are commonly referred to in instructional-design theories. These processes are described by a situated learning or a situated action theory. However, it wil be argued (in chapter 2) that instruction in which only situated activity is stimulated, may not be very effective for educational purposes. Therefore, there must be a balance between situated activity and formality in instruction. Tarski's World is believed to incorporate that balance. The main research question will address that issue: Does formal instruction, which is also stimulating situated activity, differ in effectivity from only-formal instruction or from instruction which only stimulates situated activity?

A description of Tarski's World and its research versions will be given in chapter 4. In chapter 5, the first experiments will be reported. As the expected effects were not found, instruction was strengthened by offering more explaining information. In the next experiment (chapter 6) the main research question is postponed in order to measure the effects of such added information. In the concluding and supporting experiment (chapter 7) the results from the former experiments were interpreted in reflection on the theoretical chapters 2 and 3. In chapter 8, the results will be discusssed in relation to theoretical, instructional-design and research implications.

I have no illusions about the number of people that will read this thesis from start to finish. For the very hasty readers, my suggestion would be to read at least sections 2 and 3 of chapter 2, sections 3 and 4 of chapter 4, and chapters 7 and 8. I also would like to warn readers who are merely interested in logic instruction or in an evaluation of Tarski's World: My use of Tarski's World is only instrumental in a conditional reasoning study. It does not aim at the best possible logic instruction and as far as it is an evaluation of Tarski's World, it is only a very limited one. Despite these restrictions the results have far-reaching implications for instructional science. For now Tarski's World will have to be forgotten until chapter 4, because there is much theory to work out and to describe before addressing the empirical part of this thesis.

PART I
Theory

2
The Psychology of Situated Action

2.1 What is Wrong with Cognitivism?

Situated action theory is difficult to describe without referring to its opposing paradigm, cognitivism. A review of situated action theories would include numerous highly different theories. However, all situated action theories are completely or partially opposed to fundamental assumptions of cognitivism. Therefore, the most accurate introduction to situated action theories may be a review of the assumptions and critique on cognitivism.

Main stream research in the multi-disciplinary field of cognitive science has been united by the assumption that information processing is symbolic (e.g., Gardner, 1985). This assumption leans strongly on formal logic in which deductions follow syntactic rules in order to prove the intuitions of logicians.[1] Although introspection was rejected by behaviorists, it seemed harmless to accept the introspection of logicians in which the proof seemed to be a functional representation of the line of thought during the intuition. Where introspective psychologists used imprecise and intuitive methods, logicians used stringent mathematical methods (e.g., predicate calculus) for an introspective

---

[1] Intuition is considered to be a largely unconscious induction of a thought or action, based on prior experiences.

reconstruction of their intuition. By linking such methods to behavior, a synthesis of introspection and behaviorism emerged: cognitivism.

The acceptance of a syntactic base for thought implies that the form of (internal) representation does not matter. Logicians had proved that several systems of predicate logic are equivalent, which means that each proof derived in one system can be translated into another system. Consequently, cognitive scientists did not have to worry about which representational system to use in describing human thought and action as long as it is functional. It was extremely appealing to take advantage of a representational system that could easily be implemented in another application of formal logic, a computer. In the early 70s, a production system based on if - then rules with propositions related to each other according to set theory was considered to be the functional representational system that would be able to simulate all cognitive behavior which basic function is problem solving (Newell & Simon, 1972). The computer as a model for the human mind gave also ideas for theories about memory (e.g., Schneider & Shiffrin, 1977) and learning (e.g., Anderson, 1983).

Cognitivistic theories have been very productive. Models of problem solving could be simulated, which gave rise to orthodox artificial intelligence, and memory and learning models could be empirically tested under laboratory conditions. The successes of these enterprises can be found in any general book on cognitive science (e.g., Posner, 1989) or cognitive psychology (e.g., Anderson, 1992). The main problems of cognitivistic theories were and still are psychological plausiblity and ecological validity (e.g., Neisser, 1976). Hard core cognitivists believe all there is to do is hard labor. More complex models will eventually produce the plausibility and validity needed. Other cognitivists have lost confidence in the standard logic system behind the knowledge representation systems and work out other systems based on less rigid logic systems, e.g., some kind of fuzzy logic or Bayesian logic system (e.g., Anderson, 1990). However, other researchers believe that the problems of cognitivism are irresolvable due to —for psychological purposes— ineffective logic and inappropriate epistemology. The argumentation supporting such an anti-cognitivistic position will be outlined briefly hereafter and in the next section.

The first crack in formal logic was made by Gödel who proved that there can be no complete proof procedure in logic (for a non-mathematical description see Quine, 1987, pp. 82-86): Within a formal system, it is possible to make a statement that within the system is not provable.[2] As a consequence, formal

---

[2]This paradox was (probably) foreseen by the mathematician Brouwer (Quine, 1986), who founded a radical constructivism, called intuitionism. Within intuitionism infinite sets are not accepted, because only entities that can be constructed may be postulated. This theory goes beyond mathematics, as Brouwer meant to esthablish a systematical discipline based on non-linguistic methods, dealing with *everything* (Van Dalen, 1993).

systems can either be complete or consistent but not both. Cognitivists simply ignore this devastating aspect built-in in their assumptions. And yet, even psychological research on reasoning (see chapter 3) leaves no hope for a complete and consistent syntactic theory of human reasoning. Not only proof theory is problematic, the other topic of formal logic, set theory, also presents problems to cognitivism.

Wittgenstein showed in his work on linguistic philosophy (Wittgenstein, 1953) that set theory is inappropriate for linguistic analysis. Until Wittgenstein's contribution, categories have been viewed as being unproblematic abstractions. Objects sharing certain properties, belonged to a category. Categories were believed to have clear boundaries defined by such properties. This theory was not even considered to be a theory to be debated upon or to be tested empirically. It was unanimously considered to be an unquestionable truth (Lakoff, 1987). Classical set theory is the formalization of this naive theory of categories. Wittgenstein analyzed the category *game* and concluded that it did not have clear and fixed boundaries, and that its objects constitute the category by family resemblance.[3]

As well as in philosophy and linguistics, set theory turned out to be problematic in psychology too (e.g., Rosch, Simpson & Miller, 1976; Rosch, 1978). In a series of experiments Rosch and her associates showed that (a) members of a category have asymmetric relations in similarity ratings, (b) there tend to be best-example members of categories which act as reference points, (c) Wittgenstein's family resemblance could be demonstrated, and (d) some categories are more salient than others: *basic-level categories* as opposed to superordinate or subordinate categories. They are basic in respect to perception, function, communication and knowledge organization (see Lakoff, p. 47). These findings contradict the logical view on cognition. Cognitivists have defended the symbolic representation view by a specific interpretation of Rosch's results.

Cognitivists interpreted Rosch's prototype theory as a direct reflection of an underlying representational system. In their effort to account for the prototype effects, they tried to keep set theory alive in a standard (Gleitman, Armstrong & Gleitman, 1983) or fuzzy version (Osherson & Smith, 1981) and added an error generator to it (e.g., an identification procedure). In their studies prototype effects appeared to reflect only an identification procedure, therefore prototype theory was believed to be incorrect. The critique was not very timely as Rosch had distantiated already (Rosch, 1978) from her initial position that prototype theory could be interpreted as a theory of representation or learning

---

[3]Another example is the category *polyhedron*. It has proved impossible to define these geometric objects completely (Lakatos, 1976). Each definition serves a special purpose, but there is no definition that includes all polyhedrons. Polyhedrons are used within Tarski's World (see chapter 4).

or as a processing model for categories. Rosch has been very cautious in making statements about an underlying structure or representation. Nevertheless, she assumes that prototype effects are related to a type of reasoning (Rosch, 1983).

Wittgenstein's critique and Rosch's empirical results may already be severe enough to abandon standard formal logic as the basis for a theory of cognition. Next to proof theory and set theory, semantics is troublesome too. It was Putnam (1981) who proved that model-theoretic semantics is internally inconsistent as it turned out that "the relation between symbols and the world does not characterize meaning" (Lakoff, p.229). Semantics has been recognized as a problem within psychology also as semantics of cognitivistic representations is merely intensional in nature which means that symbols only refer to other symbols instead to the entities they represent: *the symbolic fallacy* (Johnson-Laird, Herrmann & Chaffin, 1984).[4] Although the problems put forward by Wittgenstein and Putnam are still debated upon, their contributions imply at least that formal logic is *not* unproblematic for cognitive science, to put it mildly.

Based on these problems, mathematical logic including (fuzzy) set theory can be rejected as an appropriate representational tool for psychological theories of cognition as far as it dictates the structure of all knowledge. Among others, Lakoff (1987) recognized these problems as consequences of the assumption that reality is objectively knowledgeable. A knowledgeable reality means that what is considered to be the essence of reality can be taken apart or can be abstracted from the observable. The result of such abstraction is considered to be objective when it is conform to formal logic. This position may be viewed as representing a kind of realism (e.g. Lakoff, p. 159). However, when the symbolic fallacy is getting troublesome, cognitivistic ontology changes from realism (in which models of cognition refer to human activity directly) to idealism in order to save objectivity. The idealistic view on the abstracting process is that abstractions form a metaphysical level (e.g., Newell, 1982; for an overview see Anderson, 1990, p. 4) which is structured by set-theoretic relations existing independently of individual observers. Objectivists consider this level as a given to discover, not as something to construct through human understanding, although the discovery itself may be recognized as a constructive act. Within idealistic objectivism, representations (cognitivistic theories) are considered to be notational systems which do not refer to reality directly but to the metaphysical level instead. Cognitivists tend to operate on different levels of description, which allows them to be realist on one level, and idealist on another. In my

---

[4]The mental-model theory of Johnson-Laird (1983) is not a solution to this problem as it based on possible-worlds semantics which is also subject to Putnam's critique.

opinion, the objectivistic realism of cognitivists relies heavily on an idealist-logical position.

Within philosophy, no theory of logic is without troublesome debate. Consequently, there is no ground to rely on the introspections and optimism of early 20th century logicians who completed first-order predicate logic. In the next section, a Vygotskian version of situated action which does not rely on a particular logic will be worked out: the developmental situativity theory. In the following section, this theory will be compared to (a) situated cognition theory as it is known in the instructional science community, being a reaction on the formalism of contemporary education, and to (b) constructivism as it is known in the instructional science community, which is a reaction on the objectivism of contemporary education.

2.2 Situated Action

Cognitivistic models are quite successful in limited situations with well-defined research material in experiments or with well-defined problems in artificial intelligence projects. In the late seventies the low ecological validity of the results of these programs was recognized, but, reasonably, most cognitive psychologists stayed within the cognitivistic paradigm and adjusted their models in order to meet the ill-defined problems of everyday life activity. This enterprise was far less successful, and researchers in applied areas of cognitive science like instructional science (e.g., Brown, Collins & Duguid, 1989) and human computer interaction (e.g., Winograd & Flores, 1986) felt free not to wait until cognitivistic theories improved substantially and started to construct alternative theories of cognition. Also, several linguists (Lakoff, 1987), computer scientists (Clancey, 1991, Brooks, 1991a), logicians (Barwise & Perry, 1983) and anthropologists (Lave, 1988; Suchman, 1987) developed deviating theories. Within psychology, Gibson's (1966) theory of perception is an early alternative to cognitivism, a theory that has influenced Greeno (1989). Despite many differences, these theories can be grouped together as situated action theories. Proponents of situated action have made quite different, sometimes incommensurate choices in their toil towards an ecologically valid cognitive science. Below, it will be argued that situated action theories lack a psychological view that is necessary to explain the relation between situated action and the use of representations within such action. Therefore, it will be tried to construct a psychological view on situated action.

Situated Action versus Cognitivism

If there is a unifying notion behind situated action theories, it is anti-cognitivism. This may not seem to be a very strong position, but still, 'situated activists' know what they are looking for and they know that it cannot be found within cognitivism. Such intuitions, constituting an alternative *worldview* (Agre, 1993), have lead to a alternative paradigm.

What is one looking for in situated action theories? An answer can be quite straightforward when it is recognized that proponents of situated action reject the assumption that phenomena of mutual accommodation of people and the environment (physical and social) can be reduced to phenomena of people or environment taken apart (Norman, 1993). Thus, situated action theorists look for theories of mutual accommodation. Cognition or action in (most or basic) everyday life situations is considered to be unmediated by representation: The interaction of people with their environment is direct. This implies a far more important and intricate 'role' of the *context* or the *situation* in which human activity occurs than cognitivistic theories can model. The side-effect of this assumption is that there may not be a single interpretation of situated action for all research communities (Clancey, 1993). By no means does this imply that all interpretations are justified and that any inconsistency between interpretations has to be tolerated.

For psychologists who sympathize with the general notion behind situated action, there are —at least— two options to work on a situated action theory. The first option is to depart only partially from cognitivism (Greeno & Moore, 1993). This may be done by assuming invariants in the environments which do not have to be represented in order to act upon (Gibson, 1966). From this idea, theories of direct perception and direct action can be construed (Neisser, 1976; Gibson, 1986; Greeno, 1989). Only on certain occasions may symbolic processing be needed (Greeno, 1989; cf. Suchman, 1987, p. 54), for example for solving novel or difficult problems, but basically activity is situated. This view is only a partial solution to the problems of section 2.1, as Putnam's critique on semantics has not been dealt with. However, the Wittgenstein critique has been met, as logic and set theory do no longer apply to all cognition but only to special cases of processing. These cases may accord with logic and set theory.

The second and favorable option is to interpret situated action neuropsychologically (Clancey, 1993, refers to Edelman, 1992). This option is more radical than the first one and encounters many misinterpretations because the underlying worldview takes no less than a Gestalt switch before it can be understood or accepted. It may be enlightening to describe the two sides of the switch. The popular side of the switch is the physical model of the world. In this model, a clear distinction is made between an object and an observer. When an observer perceives an object, the perceived information can, reasonably, be taken to represent the object within the observer. As the representation is a representation *of* something, it can be considered to be symbolic. This view is considered to be useful and sufficient for many purposes but psychological ones.

The other side of the switch is a (neuro)psychological model of the world. In this view no distinction is made between a perception and an object, because for the observer there is only perceived information available. Therefore, psychologically —not physically— , the perceived information does not refer to the object, it *is* the object. Activity towards the object is not only based upon but also intertwines with the perceived information (i.e., the object itself). That is why activity is called *direct*. There is no symbolic layer between perception and action, between an object and an actor. There may be several processors for perceiving and acting upon objects, but these "processors coconfigure each other" during "an ongoing perception - action coordination" (Clancey, pp. 94-95). Not only an individual object is perceived and processed, but everything surrounding it. Consequently, perception of individual objects and activity towards objects is *situated*. It is within reality-as-perceived (a psychological reality) that activity occurs, not through abstracted processing of symbols.

Theories within a neuropsychological view on situated action may be formulated by neural network (or artificial neuronal network) theories, notably within robotics. These simulations of behavior have to be based on some logic system, but this system is only operative in the systems characteristics underlying perception-thought-action complexes and may be based on neurological theories. The information processed by the system is not symbolic and does not strictly follow a certain logic (although it may approximate one). Therefore, constraints on information and information processing are not determined by a timeless logic as cognitivists assume, but by changeable physical and social structures. This is a central difference between cognitivism and situated action theories. Semantical problems no longer exist as reference is not an interesting concept for non-symbolic processing, while meaning is a built-in concept.

For simulations or robotics, connectionism has been recognized as a computational pendant of situated action (Bereiter, 1991; cf. Wallner & Peschl, 1993). Connectionistic models or neural networks consist of units which stand for highly abstracted (logical) neurons. These units process information parallel, but no symbols can be found within a single unit. A stable configuration of activity over the units can be seen as equivalent to representation, but not in the sense of model-theoretic semantics as Vera and Simon (1993) do. However, apart from some promising models (Clancey, 1993, refers to Brooks, 1991b), most connectionistic models still need symbols as input and consequently they cannot be used as situated action models (except for certain purposes as will be argued later).[5]

At hand, we have a rough, rudimentary theory about situated action and a promise towards its computationability. However, in its present form, it would not go very far in describing human activity as it is evident that we do handle symbols and representations in external as well as in internal forms. No situated action theorist ignores representations or symbols functionally, but present theories lack a satisfying psychological relation between situated action and representation. To obtain this relation, two sorts of representation should be clearly differentiated —as opposed to their conflation in cognitivism—: (a) the first-order physical representation which equals the concept of *psychological reality* in situated action theory, and (b) the second-order physical representation which will be considered as a *psychological representation*. Below, an instrumental perspective on psychological representation will be worked out. However, Dewey's instrumentalism (as adhered to by Clancey, 1993) is inadequate as Vygotsky argued (1978, p. 53; see also below). It is the developmental psychology of Vygotsky that is assumed to be crucial in order to fill the psychological gap between situated action and representation. Therefore, it will be discussed in length underneath.

Vygotsky's Dynamic Bridge from Nature to Culture

> Among the most basic defects of traditional approaches [i.e. structuralism, associationism] to the study of psychology has been the isolation of the intellectual from the volitional and affective aspects of consciousness. The inevitable consequence of the isolation of these functions has been the transformation of thinking into an autonomous stream. Thinking itself became the thinker of thought. Thinking was divorced from the full vitality of life, from the motives, interests, and inclinations of the thinking individual (Vygotsky, 1934/1987, p. 50).

Contrary to the main stream psychology of his time and beyond, Vygotsky assumed the existence of "a dynamic meaningful system that constitutes a unity of affective and intellectual processes" (Vygotsky, p. 50). This very complex system does not simply unfold during maturation, but it develops primarily through social interaction. By following the process of ontogenetic development, Vygotsky's ideas may begin to become intelligible. This process may be

---

[5]As most neural network researchers are technology driven and therefore hardly concerned with psychological constraints and requirements on their models, an extensive and thorough analysis of what is needed for a situated action theory must present such constraints and requirements.

described as a development in stages, but Vygotsky saw this stage theory merely as a useful artifact of his experimental methods. In reality, development is a continuous process comprising of numerous transitional stages which are not clearly seperated. The following description of Vygotsky's theory is based on Vygotsky and Luria (1994) and Vygotsky (1987, 1978).

The newborn child perceives and acts upon perceptions in a conflated manner: Perception is an integral aspect of motor actions. The motives of the infant are related to the possibilities of objects (compare with Gibson's affordances) as if they dictate what must be done: e.g., to throw or grab small things, or later, to climb a staircase, and to open and close doors. Consequently, motivation, perception, and action are integrated. This means that action is constrained by the situation in which the infant finds him or herself, that it is captured in the natural field of perception (i.e., the psychological reality). The infant's activity starts as simple grasping for objects or *gestures-in-itself*, which are unmediated (no tools, persons or symbols are used). But soon problems arise: some interesting objects cannot be reached. Now the infant discovers that the gesture triggers other persons to get the object. The gesture-in-itself becomes a *gesture-for-others*. It may also discover that certain available objects can be used as tools to reach wanted objects that are too far away. This is the start of instrumental or *practical intelligence*. Thinking here is completely bound to the situation, using tools or other persons, but no symbols yet.

In the mean time, the child learns to speak, but the words' function is only indicative and nominative. For the child, the word is part of the object. Speech is a social activity without intelligence while thought has no verbal aspects: speech and thought are not related yet. Speech first follows action (e.g., an object can only be named after drawing it as if labels can only be used when objects are visible). A crucial development is action accompanied by speech. The child, confronted with a practical problem, does not only use eyes and hands, but also speech to solve it. First, speech is directed to other persons, but soon speech is turned to the child itself. It becomes *egocentric*. Words are produced by the child towards itself as if it were another being, regarding itself as an object. From this activity inner motivations will develop; motivation will no longer be exclusively external (i.e., driven from objects), but will also be driven by words. Through egocentric speech a child eventually begins to master its own behavior. Speech creates, parallel to the stimuli of the environment, a second series of stimuli standing between the child and its environment and directing its behavior. By the use of symbols the child acquires a relative freedom from the situation that directly attracts it, and impulsive attempts are transformed into a more planned, organized behavior.

The source of individual intelligent behavior, therefore, is the application of a social attitude to itself. However, not practical problems but play is the vital activity for the child to emancipate from situational constraints. Within play, the child learns to detach meaning from objects. This is not an easy or automatic process. Only special objects may be given the meaning that belongs to other objects (e.g., a stick, but certainly not a postcard, may be given the meaning 'horse'). As the child does not accept free substitution of meanings to objects, play is not symbolism. All play comprises imaginary situations, but within early play there is little of the imaginary. Early play is hardly more than a memory in action, one that is not clearly separated from the real situation. Through play, creative activities like drawing, and practical problems the child is gradually learning to sever meaning from objects, clearing the way for motives to become *intentions*. Thinking, then, is not merely activity on a practical plane, but has merged with egocentric speech, and later with internalized (or inner) speech, in order to precede and guide action. The child is no longer captured by a demanding *space* at present, but is structuring its situation purposefully in *time* (past, present, and future) too, or in Vygotsky's (Vygotsky & Luria, 1994, p. 122) own words:

> At the moment when, thanks to the planning assistance of speech, a view of the future is included as an active agent, the child's whole operational psychological field changes radically and its behaviour is fundamentally reconstructed. The child's perception begins to develop according to new laws that differ from those of the natural optical field. The fusion of sensory and motor fields is overcome, and the spontaneous impulsive actions with which it responded to each stimulus appearing in the optic field and attracting it, is now restrained. The child's attention begins to function in a new way, while its memory from a passive 'registrator' becomes a function of active selection and intellectual recollection.

This new flexible field of attention creates the well-known possibilities of memory, planning, reasoning, etc. However, Vygotsky (Vygotsky & Luria, p. 140) assures us that

> The higher psychological functions are not super-imposed as a second storey over the elementary processes, but represent new psychological systems which include a complex knot of elementary functions that, upon being included in the new system, begin to act according to new laws. Each higher psychological function thus presents a unity of higher order, determined mainly by the particular combination of a series of more elementary functions in a new whole.

Now, the bridge between action and speech, between the biological and the cognitive functions, or between nature and culture has been described in broad lines. It is clear that it is a very complex bridge, changing both itself during the construction as well as the parts to be bridged. It is not based on a single logical formula with an unchangeable number of variables with fixed parameters. It is a bridge first constructed in phylogenetic history and rebuild personally within the scaffold of a socio-historic environment.[6]

The concepts used in action and speech also follow a development. Therefore, some notions of Vygotsky on concept formation and word meaning should be mentioned. Vygotsky's most important contribution to concept formation theory is his rejection of positions claiming that the acquisition of formal concepts is merely a deductive (top down) or merely an inductive (bottom up) process: A child cannot simply discover formal concepts or simply reach a symbolic attitude to stimuli through intuition. Both positions dispose metaphysically of the question of the genesis of symbolic activity. Vygotsky's proposal runs as follows. The development of concepts starts, naturally, with the infant. As soon as the infant is able to distinguish objects, perceptions are generalized to groups of objects. This first categorization is no more than an unstable and diffuse feeling towards objects. The connection of this affective perception with words learned through social interaction gives the word meaning. This grouping of objects is highly subjective, it may be based on trial-and-error connections that have no function in the social world. The child gradually learns to select more 'objective' or socially agreeable connections. When a perceptual generalization reflects features which are also recognized by adults, it has reached a new structure: *complexes*. Complexes are not logical abstractions, but instead non-hierarchical, concrete and factual connections based on several kinds of associations, amongst which are family-like associations. Clearly, Vygotsky already has in mind the Wittgenstein-Rosch concept of family resemblance. Especially the vague, diffuse complexes of familial unity of things is important for further concept development as they include inherently limitless possibilities of extension. Some extensions are beyond the limits of the concrete world, beyond the domain of practical thinking. Complexes with such extensions are, ultimately, the basis for formal concepts.

The development of perceptual generalizations and complexes is basically inductive, even though the speech of adults —and the child's egocentric

---

[6]There is an analogy between the phylo- and ontogenesis of DNA (or RNA) and the phylo- and ontogenesis of intentions. DNA researchers have a good picture of how DNA is constructed ontogenetically. Already existing complex enzymes help to form new DNA string. The real problem, therefore, is transported to the start of phylogenetic history: How does life start, how does the first string of molecules copy itself? Vygotsky put forward where to look for an answer of the intentional problem. It is not yet as clear as the DNA-genesis, but there is a start: It is the socio-cultural environment which triggers a socio-cultural development. However, even when this ontogenetic development of psychological functions is clear, we will have to find an answer for the phylogenetic genesis of intention.

speech— is needed for developing complexes. This line of 'spontaneous' development is what Vygotsky called *everyday concepts* development, which can easily be compared to basic-level concepts (e.g., Rosch, 1978; Bereiter, 1992). Vygotsky proposed a second line of concept development, concerning *scientific or formal concepts* (compare this to the dual reasoning system of Rosch, 1983, one for prototypes and one for formal reasoning). Formal concepts develop non-spontaneously, meaning that formal instruction —a top-down process— is required. This process, like the everyday concept development, starts from the early days of childhood (as parents and other adults use abstract concepts in their communication with children), but the real spin-off is at school. Formal concepts must be based on an already available system of (initially everyday) concepts. Its genesis is from those complexes which are phenotypically identical to formal concepts (pseudo concepts) to the real formal concepts. At this point, (i.e., the development from pseudo to real concepts), I will take leave from Vygotsky, as he seems to hold an objectivistic position, which claims that reality has timeless inner relations which can be objectivated in a set-theoretic system of concepts. However, even when it would be accepted, it does not mean that we, human beings, can ultimately and completely reach this metaphysical level of concepts and can afford to leave the swamps of everyday concepts, as Vygotsky clearly sees the weakness of the formal concept:

> The weakness of the everyday concept lies in its incapacity for abstraction. [...] In contrast, the weakness of the scientific concept lies in its verbalism, in its insufficient saturation with the concrete (Vygotsky, 1987, p. 169).

In everyday life, therefore, we will mostly use everyday concepts.

A final word about meaning, one of the central problems of cognitive science. Meaning, as it changes and develops, is not something that can be logically reconstructed (semantics) after a syntactic analysis of concepts, but instead Vygotsky poses it as the unit of analysis itself. This is the consequence of Vygotsky's rejection of the still popular idea that the elements of verbal thinking —speech and thinking— can be separated for psychological analysis as the characteristics of the two elements differ from the characteristics of the whole. The cognitive scientist who sees no problem in doing this, is compared by Vygotsky to a researcher who tries to explain why water extinguishes fire from its elements oxygen and hydrogen (p. 244). Meaning lies in the unity of a symbol system (e.g., inner speech) and thinking. The relation of thought to word changes in development (which is functional, not age-related). The relation is not a static logical one, but a process. Even within a single event there is a movement from thought to word and from word to thought. Therefore, thought is not expressed, but completed in the word. Thought is not the source of our behavior, as the following quotation of Vygotsky shows. Now, a situated action theory can be further developed both incorporating a psychological perspective on concept formation as well as avoiding the problems described in section 2.1.

> Thought has its origin in the motivating sphere of consciousness, a sphere that includes our inclinations and needs, our interests and impulses, and our affect and emotion. The affective and volitional tendency stands behind thought (Vygotsky, p. 282).

Formality in Situated Action: The Developmental Situativity Theory

The concept of symbols as tools for thought is a compelling and powerful one in situated action theories (e.g., Clancey, 1993), but Vygotsky warns us that symbols, in contrast to instrumental, physical tools, are not catalysts. The use of symbolic tools may change the information-processing (or activation) structure and its possibilities and consequently the meaning of the symbols themselves. However, in my view, this holds only for the symbols of everyday concepts as used in situated action. Within the other Vygotskian line of concept formation, the development of formal concepts, the use of symbols is catalytic: During its use, a formal concept does not alter the information processing (or activation) structure.

My interpretation of Vygotsky's findings is that children, in their early use of concepts (although words appear to refer to formal concepts, they are actually bound to everyday concepts, complexes), are trying to situate formal concepts. This hopeless effort, however, enhances their ability for generalization (a concrete, situated sort of generalization, which is not synonymous to abstraction), which leads to Vygotsky's psuedo concepts.[7] The difference between pseudo concepts and real, formal concepts, he argues, is merely understanding. Eventually, the child, now an adolescent, will understand abstract, formal concepts. In my view, the crucial understanding of the adolescent does not concern formal concepts itself, instead it is a more general, not-necessarily conscious insight (or even an attitude) that formal concepts are not truly meant

---

[7]For example, the mathematical formula $y = ax + b$: Students may try to situate this formula by substituting the constants with numbers and the variables with a range of numbers as is possible within the external representation technique used (e.g., a coordinate system on a blackboard). The effort is hopeless because the representation of a single instantiation is always inadequate (the line is finite and has a certain thickness). Students learn that it does not matter how far and thick the line is drawn and that the materials on which the representation is drawn are insignificant. Students may thus acquire a *pseudo concept* of the formula.

to be understood at all, at least not in the sense of the fully affective or situated understanding of everyday concepts. This insight opens the way to the adolescent for a pragmatism towards symbols, a tools perspective. Not that affect or situated action does not play any role in this insight, but it is not coupled as direct and complete to the used symbols as is the case with everyday concepts. Instead, it is mostly limited to the purpose, the intention of the act itself. The intention and control of formal thinking is well rooted in situated action. This provides formal thinkers with the feeling that they understand what they are doing, even when the meaning of the elements of the process is kept minimal. The meaning of the (intermediate) result of the thought, a symbol or a symbol system, has to be reconstructed, i.e., situated. But this reconstruction is only partial, as abstractions simply cannot be situated completely.[8] There is no harm in this, as the thinker only had instrumental intentions with the formal act.

Although instrumental, at least part of the formality should have a meaningful relation to the situated sphere of everyday concepts. Through this relation, the use of formal concepts changes situated action itself. This implies that humans' perception of reality —the psychological reality— may not only change during the development of everyday concepts, which is a fully affective, situated development, but also through the instrumental use of formal concepts.[9] The *real* reality, which may be assumed to exist without our perception, is not objectively knowledgeable, as it can only be known through the senses, i.e., through a changing situated action. The psychological reality is a dynamic personal construction based on social and physical interaction. The function of everyday concepts is to control the personal psychological reality, the function of formal concepts is to control (religiously, politically or scientifically) the unknown, real reality, or at least attempt to control it by a psychological representation.

The situated action theory presented in this section is conceived as providing a psychological relation of situated action and formal symbol systems by means of Vygotsky's developmental psychology. It will be referred to as the *developmental situativity theory* in the remainder of this thesis. Situativity is a term coined by Greeno and Moore (1993) to avoid the reference to action or to cognition (as in situated action or situated cognition). Situativity is not a *type* of motor action or cognition, instead it is assumed to be a general characteristic of

---

[8]Logicians tried to abstract this formal thinking in the most rigid way. The resulting logic has proved useful for some purposes, but its semantics can never be reconstructed to the full psychological scale (Vygotsky, 1934/1987; Putnam, 1981). Hence the impossible mission of the cognitivists.

[9]This use of formal symbols is still instrumental or catalytic, because the change of a person's reality is happening only through the situated mode of acting. However, the next, again instrumental use of the symbol may not be the same as before.

all information processing (there is no clear distinction between perception, cognition, and action). Here, the term development encompasses both the global structural changes during childhood as well as very specific learning processes (e.g., in adults).

2.3 Instructional Design and the Developmental Situativity Theory

By the end of the 80s, two important notions in the field of instructional science gave the impetus to reactions to formal education: situated cognition and constructivism. In this section it will be demonstrated that the integration of these notions in the developmental situativity theory as described above provides for a radically different view on instruction than separate treatments do.

Situated cognition, as it was put forward by Brown, Collins & Duguid (1989), is the notion that knowledge or concepts are bound to activities in situations. In everyday life, this activity is authentic. Authentic activity is meaningful, coherent and purposeful in a concrete social or cultural environment. If we need concepts, they are used as tools, they do not constitute or determine activity itself. The problem with education, as being largely formal, is that it presupposes that knowledge is detachable from authentic activities, that we are able to store and retrieve it in such detachable structures, and that we are able to use it under certain appropriate conditions (which may be learned by several concrete examples). The situated cognition idea rejects these assumptions. It considers formal education institutions as environments with their own cultural significance in which activity aimed at the acquisition of knowledge is not authentic. Knowledge is not bound to meaningful activities, but instead to reading textbooks, listening to teachers, and doing exercises. This inauthentic use of knowledge has limited use outside the borders of schools and universities. As an authentic alternative to formal education, Brown et al. (1989) propose *cognitive apprenticeship*, in which students are encultured by activity and social interaction in authentic cognitive tasks, analogous to craft apprenticeship. In short, situated cognition emphasizes the idea of an active, experiencing student in a situation where knowledge is not transmitted to the student, but constructed through activity or social interaction. When one emphasizes the constructive element in this process, one may end up as an educational constructivist.

Constructivism, introduced to the field of instructional science by Jonassen (1991), is the notion that reality is a personal or social invention or construction. Where situated cognition emphasizes the environmental role in knowledge, constructivists emphasize the construction of knowledge. The problem with formal education, then, is that knowledge is imposed on the student and it is expected, or hoped for, that knowledge will have identical meaning for each individual. Educational constructivists propose education in which students find more opportunity to construct their own knowledge. Hence the *open learning environments*, in which students can structure their ideas (which is something like formalization of intuitions) about any subject. There may be environments (see Duffy, Lowyck & Jonassen, 1993) based on negotiation (e.g., Bubble dialogue), or environments in which students may structure their ideas in specific knowledge structures, as for example semantic networks (SemNet).

As the notions of situated cognition and constructivism clearly have much in common with the developmental situativity theory, it is remarkable that instructional design stemming from those notions do not look like anything of the possible instructional design that may be developed on the basis of the developmental situativity theory (see also section 8.4). It is important to have a close look at the differences between the developmental situativity theory and situated cognition on the one hand and constructivism on the other.

The main difference between the developmental situativity theory and situated cognition is the lack of psychology in the latter. In the perception of instructional scientists, there can only be situated cognition when the learning situation has obvious authenticity. Consequently, situated cognition is a function of external, non-psychological variables. Such task-level definition of situated cognition implies that no assumptions of information processing are made. Although situated cognition researchers may see the limits of cognitivistic symbolic information processing, they may see no harm in using cognitivistic models eclectically. The developmental situativity theory, however, clearly rejects all symbolic processing, although some information processing may resemble symbolic processing (especially when symbolic tools are used in a sequence). Not only does the lack of psychological assumptions limit the instructional possibilities for situated learning, some forms of authentic tasks or collaboration may have very little or no situated action at all for the learner (e.g., the instructional subject matter of this thesis: formal logic). Without a developmental (including learning) psychology, it will be harder to determine which tasks are appropriate.

Constructivists do not make any difference between the construction of a psychological reality and the construction of the real reality (i.e., a psychological representation). They do not distinguish between the use of everyday concepts and the use of formal concepts. However, this difference is important as the meaning-saturation for both types of concepts differs (everyday concepts are always used in fully meaningful instantiations, whereas formal concepts are used in abstraction, which can only be indirectly and partially meaningful). When constructivists are equating construction of reality with construction of knowledge, they are not referring to the psychological reality (even though this reality is constructed through the use of symbols for everyday concepts). Instead, constructed knowledge as conceived by constructivists is an idiosyncratic type of *formal* knowledge in a clear, structural representation. As with situated cognition, the problem of constructivism is the lack of psychology. It remains a mystery how such abstract representations are meaningful or experienced. When this is not clear, it is not a comfortable thought that we all have different representations, or different meanings for the same representation. Constructivists have to explain how it is possible that we normally do seem to have pretty much the same notions of (at least everyday) concepts. Jonassen (1992) explains that we construct meaning through social negotiation. After this long process we often have roughly the same meaning for a representation. Roughly, because there will always remain individual differences. "If you don't believe me", Jonassen provokes us, "try to get a group of people to agree on the critical attributes of a 'chair'" (p. 144). Now this is interesting as it demonstrates that constructivists (or only in Jonassen's construction?) *are* aiming at formal concepts for their construction of reality. I will not dispute the difficulty of defining a chair, but instead state another question: 'Try to find a person who fails to recognize a newly designed chair as being a chair'. The person must have a major brain damage or disturbance to fail recognition, or the designer must have designed a pretty unfunctional chair (in which case most people would call it a piece of art, not a chair). My point is that the meaning of everyday concepts is very similar among people (within a culture), even though the formation of everyday concepts may have been a long constructive way.

The function of formal concepts, as conceived in situated action, is to control the real world, that is, the reality that cannot be understood by everyday concepts, the reality beyond the personal world. This reality is normally not constructed by oneself or constructed through negotiation (therefore, open learning environments are not very useful). It is a reality which must be taught (cf. Bereiter, 1992), which means *re*constructed (indeed not transmitted). When there are several important viewpoints or symbol systems, then several important viewpoints have to be taught. When the contemporary viewpoint is not disputed, there is one viewpoint to be taught (of course former viewpoints may still be interesting or enhance the acceptation of the new one). Formal concepts are instrumental, their meaning may be reconstructed partially and different persons may reconstruct different meanings. This is not very important as long as students have the feeling that they understand the matter, and there are no signs that they use the concepts differently. The *construction* of those formal systems is done by creative (and influential) religious leaders, politicians or scientists. It is not a bad thing when society asks educational institutions to impose the contemporary or stable symbol systems to students. However, it is a bad thing when teachers pretend that they teach unquestionable truths as they only teach useful constructions, and it is also a bad thing when instruction leaves no opportunity to reconstruct the imposed construction. For the reconstruction of formal constructions, it is needed to understand how meaningful processing of information works. The developmental situativity theory is a start for such understanding.

3

The Psychology of Deductive Reasoning

3.1 The Questions of Competence, Bias, and Content

Since the middle of the 19th century, when philosophers clearly began to sever the psychology of thinking from the study of logic, the latter has been taken as a normative theory of reasoning, whereas the former has been concerned with the extent to which people actually reason in line with logic. Looking backwards, three central questions in the psychological study on deductive reasoning can be distinguished: (a) the competence question, (b) the bias question and (c) the content question (Evans, Newstead & Byrne, 1993).

The *competence question* reflects the fact that people appear to be able to reason (not merely rely on memory) as they make logical choices above chance level in tasks. Despite such competence, people make many errors in reasoning tasks. Many errors are systematic as different subjects often make the same type of errors (biases) in different tasks. The *bias question* is concerned with the factors causing such biases. Naturally, one speaks of competence, errors and biases from the normative perspective of logic. This may not do justice to human rationality as not all logical reasoning tasks are relevant in everyday life. Rationality does not necessarily need to be defined as a *rationality of process* in which reasoning itself should be logical, but instead it may be defined as a *rationality of purpose* in which people try to achieve personal (Evans, 1993) or even evolutionary (Anderson, 1990) goals. When we assume that people are rational in the latter definition, the role of content and context in relevant reasoning will be apparent. Indeed, the content of the reasoning problems and the context in which the problems appear, do influence responses strongly. The *content question* is about those features of problem content and context that effect the reasoning process of subjects.

In this chapter a brief review of findings and theories of conditional reasoning researchwill be provided (partly following the extensive review of Evans et al., 1993). The situated action perspective does not yet provide for an explicit theory of reasoning, but it will be argued that the development of competence is a neglected but important aspect of the competence question.

3.2 Conditional Reasoning

The Wason Selection Task

Nearly three decenniums ago Wason (1966) presented the field of psychology of thinking with an elegant conditional reasoning task that became famous as the Wason selection task. The selection task is credited for the most important research paradigm in the psychology of human reasoning (e.g., Evans et al., 1993). Many versions of the selection task have been constructed, but the standard abstract version is as follows. Subjects are given four cards with a letter or a number on each card, for instance 'A', '2', 'F', and '5'. Subjects are told that on each card there is a number on one side and a letter on the other. A rule says that:

> If there is an 'A' on one side of the card,
> then there is a '5' on the other side.

The subject now has to select only those cards necessary to determine the correctness of the rule. The card with an 'A' should be selected as there must be a '5' on the other side as the rule supposes. The card with a '2' must also be examined because when an 'A' is found on the other side it falsifies the rule. The other cards are not informative.

The logic behind the selection task is elementary. The *if P then Q* rule can be abstracted to the *material implication* $P \rightarrow Q$. P and Q can be any statement. The semantics of those statements are reduced to truth values (true or false). The meaning of the connective is also reduced to truth-functionality. The truth function of the material implicator ($\rightarrow$) says that a statement $P \rightarrow Q$ is true except when the *antecedent* (statement P) is true and the *consequent* (statement Q) is false (see Figure 3.1). This implies that in (standard) logic, statements do

P	Q	P → Q
T	T	T
T	F	F
F	T	T
F	F	T

Figure 3.1. Truth table for the material implication in first-order logic. P and Q are statements. T and F stand for the truth values true and false. The first column presents truth values of the statements. The second column provides for the truth value of the conditional that may be derived given the truth values of P and Q.

not relate to each other in terms of, e.g., causality or temporality. This semantical reduction is important for mathematical operations as natural semantics of statements is often ambiguous. Logic is especially powerful because a line of thought can be set up fully in syntactic operations. As syntactic operations are not subjective, ambiguous, or affective, the line of thought can be readily accepted as a proof that a statement is true or false.

Elementary rules in a proof are the modus ponens and the modus tollens. The *modus ponens* holds that when the implication P → Q and the statement P are given, Q can be derived. The *modus tollens* holds that when the implication P → Q and the negation of statement Q (not-Q) are given, P is false (not-P). In the selecton task with the rule *if there is an 'A' on one side of the card then there is a '5' on the other side* choosing the 'A' card (a true antecedent) is applying the modus ponens as there must be a '5' on the other side of the card (consequent must be true) when the implication is true. Choosing the '2' card (a false consequent) is applying the modus tollens as there should not be an 'A' on the other side of the '2' card (antecedent must be false) when the implication is true. Both rules have to be applied in order to be able to falsify the conditional in a selection task.

Despite the elementary logic needed for solving the selection task, most studies report that only about ten percent of the subjects solve the task. In general, nearly all subjects apply the modus ponens rule, but most subjects fail to apply the modus tollens. In addition to the modus ponens, a substantial percentage of subjects choose the '5' card (a true consequent), wrongly assuming that the antecedent must be true too (the *fallacy of affirming the consequent*). Logically, this is an irrelevant choice as the implication is true whether the antecedent is true or false. The other irrelevant choice is not chosen very often: the 'F' card (a false antecedent; wrongly assuming that the consequent must be false too: the *fallacy of denying the antecedent*). The combined results of four early experiments (Johnson-Laird & Wason, 1970) gives the following typical percentages: 33 percent of subjects apply the modus ponens rule only, 46 percent of the subjects apply the fallacy of affirming the consequent in addition to the modus ponens, 4 percent apply the modus tollens as well as the modus ponens and the remaining 17 percent of the subjects make other combinations of choices.

This early research on the selection task was somewhat disappointing as it proved that intelligent adults do not reason in line with standard formal logic. Truly surprising was the finding that attempts of varying strengths to cue subjects to the importance of the modus tollens hardly improve logical reasoning. A cue may even be a full explanation in which subjects are made aware of their logical errors in earlier selection tasks, or literally prompting that an 'A' on the back of a '2' card would falsify the rule! Evans et al. (1993) conclude that these studies demonstrate "a markedly persistent logical error on an apparently simple task which is difficult to eliminate" (p. 103).

Several research lines have been set up to investigate whether the content or the context of the rules would have a facilitating effect. Although thematic and task-instructional effects are not of particular interest for our purpose, some findings should be mentioned in order to understand the theories described in the next part of this section. The standard selection task is often described as abstract, in contrast to tasks with concrete rules which may be called realistic or thematic. For the research in this thesis a different discrimination is important: one between arbitrary and familiar selection tasks. Arbitrary tasks do not provide any cue, in contrast to familiar tasks in which some kind of memory process may be activated by its content or context. Arbitrary tasks can be abstract or concrete, but familiar tasks will have a concrete content.

A well-known example of a thematic effect involving a memory process is the Postal rule (Johnson-Laird, Legrenzi & Legrenzi, 1972; Griggs & Cox, 1982). A Postal rule may be stated as follows: 'If the letter is sealed than it has a 50 lire stamp on it'. In some countries, sealed envelopes are more expensive to mail than unsealed envelopes. Subjects who are familiar with such a postal rule make more often correct choices than subjects who are unfamiliar with it (88 against 57 percent, Cheng & Holyoak, 1985).

Yachanin and Tweney (1982) tried to explain the facilitating effects of thematic content by the accompanying instruction of the task. They believed that the instructional context of thematic rules cued subjects to search for violations of the rule whereas the standard selection task merely invites subjects to find out whether the rule is true or false. After a series of experiments it is concluded (Evans et al, 1993) that violation instruction by itself does not effect reasoning, but it may enhance an already facilitative effect of thematic content.

A stronger contextual effect is provided by instruction that eliminates a special kind of ambiguity of the task. Margolis (1987, referred to by Griggs,

1989) argues that people in everyday life deal with things in context and not as detached puzzles. People are usually free to decide *how* to handle a (new) problem. Margolis labels these situations as open scenario's. These scenarios may close after some experience with it. The Wason selection task, in contrast, is a new but already closed scenario: How to act in it is limited to an imposed choice within a constrained set of possibilities. Although subjects know they have to make a choice with four particular cards, they will be tempted to see (tacitly) the task as an open scenario because they have no experience with it. Margolis calls this *scenario ambiguity*. The result is that subjects tend to see a card not as a specific card, but as a symbol referring to a category. For example, subjects tend to interpret the 'A' card in the rule above as standing for all possible 'A' cards. Consequently, only selecting the 'A' card is sufficient to falsify the rule as it is an exhaustive search for counter examples.[1] Griggs (1989) tested and supported Margolis' theory by using an arbitrary rule in a familiar closed scenario context (using playing cards). The result was that 50 percent of the subjects applied the modus ponens as well as the modus tollens.

Margolis' notion of scenario ambiguity is important for explaining some findings of the abstract selection task. However, feedback on the subjects' performance and explanations or direct cues concerning the selection tasks should be sufficient to remove the ambiguity. As this is not the case, scenario ambiguity can only be a partial explanation. There are several other partial explanations which will be described underneath.

Theories of Reasoning

In the 60s and 70s the experimental findings that drove the questions of competence, bias and content were so intriguing and difficult that reasoning researchers were rather isolated from the main stream cognitive psychology of that time. The competence question was hardly an issue in cognitive psychology in that period: The central processor of the human brain was assumed to be a standard logical processor. Researchers who were interested in how people actually think, could build an error generator in the model to account for structural empirical deviations. This position can also be found in the early days of the psychology of reasoning in the form of the strongest version of what is

---

[1]This theory also provides for an explanation of the selection of P and Q cards (in a rule: if P then Q), when assuming that the subjects who select P and Q cards interpret the rule as a bi-conditional (e.g., Staudenmayer, 1975). This selection would be erronous in itself as the correct response for a biconditional would be the selection of all four cards. However, when a subject sees the cards as categories for a bi-conditional statement, only P and Q selections are needed.

called the formal rule or mental logic theory (Henle, 1962). This theory and its alternatives will here be described in very general lines. For specific experimental findings or theoretical arguments, pro or contra, see Evans et al. (1993). It should be noted that many findings were acquired through other research paradigms than the selection task.

There are several *formal rule* theories, but they all assume an inherent mental logic comprising of a set of abstract inference rules or schema's. As these rules are abstract they can be applied in all contexts in the same syntactic way. Henle's (1962) version of this theory is the strongest as the inference rules are identical to the rules of formal logic. She believed that reasoning errors are mainly consequences of misinterpretation of the reasoning task. Piaget's developmental psychology (Inhelder & Piaget, 1958) can also be positioned as a strong -mathematical logic- version of mental logic. Apart from misinterpretation, errors may occur in children because the mental logic system has not unfolded itself yet. Adults should be able to reason logically, but there may have been developmental problems during their childhood causing bad reasoning habits. The critique on these strong versions of mental logic was that serious that they have been abandoned since the early 70s (Falmagne, 1975a; for a review see Evans, 1982).

Later versions of mental logic are logically less complete, e.g., missing the modus tollens as an inherent rule. The human proof system may not be like predicate calculus, but more like natural deduction (a proof system used by logicians for purposes to which the better known predicate calculus is less comfortable), which is actually logically equivalent to predicate calculus but appears to be more natural (Osherson, 1975; Braine, 1978). Some of these versions may also be less formal than standard logic in the sense that the inference rules do not transcend a certain mode of representation, notably a natural linguistic one (Falmagne, 1975b). Even though inference rules are believed to be inborn, children may need to learn the words 'and', 'or', and 'if' before using these connectives and applying the modus ponens (Falmagne, 1990; Braine, 1990). According to Braine (1990), a *natural logic* consists primarily of universal and automatic reasoning skills, but, in addition, more complex reasoning skills may be acquired. Many critiques on natural logics, Braine argues, result from not distinguishing the primary, phylogenetic reasoning skills from the secondary, ontogenetic ones, which may be content-sensitive (Rips, 1989; Braine & O'Brien, 1991). The critique Braine refers to, stems from researchers who were more attracted to the bias and content questions than to the competence question.

In the early 80s many researchers believed that most responses to logical reasoning tasks did not reflect reasoning competence, but other cognitive processes instead, especially involving memory processes (Mankletow & Evans,

1979; Griggs & Cox, 1982). This is called the *availability theory* of content effects. This theory explains nicely, for example, the Postal rule described above. Availability theory is no longer very attractive as it has been absorbed by a more complex hybrid theory, incorporating elements of formal rule theory as well as availability theory: reasoning schema theories. The idea of a reasoning schema theory is that through experiencing certain types of familiar rules (e.g., the Postal rule), people may induce reasoning schema's. Reasoning schema's may have been induced ontogenetically (*Pragmatic Reasoning Schema's*, Cheng & Holyoak, 1985) or phylogenetically (*Social Contracts*, Cosmides, 1989). An example of a pragmatic reasoning schema is the permission schema: 'If an action is to be taken then a precondition must be satisfied' (Cheng, Holyoak, Nisbett & Oliver, 1986). Reasoning schema's are abstract, but not as abstract as the material conditional because the antecedent is deontically related to the consequent.

Apart from (generalized) memory processes, another non-reasoning process, *motivation*, may as well play a role in logical reasoning tasks. When subjects believe a rule (as used, e.g., in a selection task) is false, they may be motivated to disprove it. Motivation may determine the relevance of choices. *Relevance* may concern outcomes which satisfy a need or have positive utility (George, 1991) or it may concern choices which are subjectively judged to have a high chance to occur (Kirkby, 1994).

All the theories mentioned so far are rather specific theories or they can only explain some of the many empirical findings. The theory that can claim to account for the widest variety of deductive phenomena is the *mental model* theory of Johnson-Laird (1983). Johnson-Laird originally proposed his theory to account for syllogistic reasoning, but recently the theory has been applied to the domains of meta-deduction, and propositional, quantificational, and relational inference (see Evans et al., 1993, for a review). The idea behind mental model theory is that it emphasizes the extensional semantical nature of representations in contrast to the only-intensional semantics of formal rule theories. Symbols may be defined intensionally by their relation to other symbols, but their relation to reality, to the entities that are referred to, remains unclear. A mental model is believed to be a representation which has a structure analogous to reality, implying that extensional semantics has been established for the representation. Reasoning with mental models is possible through (yet unclear) transformation procedures directed towards finding counterexamples.

Evans et al. (1993) conclude their review by stating that the field of deductive reasoning is in a good, healthy shape and that in the last decade new theories (mental model theory and reasoning schema theory) were developed from scratch and these theories are, instead of the isolated reasoning theories of the

60s and 70s, at the core of cognitive science. Despite this positive conclusion, the field of deductive reasoning is rather fragmented, and the arguments between the positions can hardly be expected to be resolved in the near future. Yet, for the research in this thesis it is important to find out which position in the field of deductive reasoning is (a) interesting from the perspective of the developmental situativity theory and (b) which is relevant for the research questions described in chapter 1.

With the criticism on cognitivistic theories (see section 2.1) in mind, it can be argued that the formal rule theories and the mental model theory are least compatible to situated action theory. These theories reflect two sides of the same logical coin: a syntactic (proof theoretic) and a semantic (model-theoretic) side. As long as a formal logic is used for constraining representational theories, whatever side of logic they stress, such theories will inherently have a troublesome relation to reality (see Putnam, 1981). For that reason, the focus will be on pragmatic theories of reasoning as a reference point, even though there may be several important and useful elements in natural logics or in mental model theory.

Pragmatic reasoning schema theory is also interesting as it is the only reasoning theory paying explicit attention to learning. Other reasoning theories are pessimistic, unclear, or even negative about possibilities for improvement of human reasoning skill. In contrast, the developmental situativity theory is quite positive for learning to reason logically, provided that some conditions are met. Tarski's World has been developed especially to ensure that students learn the semantic aspects of logic. Among these aspects is the meaning of the material conditional, which, as shown above, subjects generally do not recognize in arbitrary Wason selection tasks. In the next chapter it will be argued that Tarski's World does meet the conditions specified by the developmental situativity theory and consequently, it should be possible to find a training effect of Tarski's World on the selection task. But first, the learning assumptions of pragmatic reasoning schema theory will be discussed.

3.3 Learning to Reason: A Pragmatic View

Pragmatic Reasoning Schema's are rules which are more abstract than concrete rules, but not entirely abstract. Such schema's are assumed to be induced by experiencing the effects when rules are applied. This abstraction process is described by Holland, Holyoak, Nisbett, and Thagard (1986) in their *induction framework*. This set of theories, all reflecting some aspect of induction, was constructed to describe real life learning processes computationally. Central to induction, as conceived by Holland et al., is the notion of a flexible rule-based system that is constrained by pragmatic goals and has experiences as input. Despite their concern with reality and experience —which contrasted with most rule-based systems of that time— and the analogy to connectionistic models, the framework stayed within a cognitivist tradition. That is, representations are considered to be built from elementary symbolic entities and all further processing is considered to remain symbolic. The argumentation for it, however, is to a large extent technical and pragmatic. Later work (e.g., Thagard, 1989; for a review see Holyoak & Spellman, 1993) is explicitly connectionistic, although it still depends on symbolic input.

The induction framework may be described easiest in terms of production rules. As a representation never fully reflects the situation it represents, there is always some probabilistic element in it. A model of a situation is defined as a set of rules which may be more or less abstract, depending on earlier experiences. Each application of a model to a new situation may strengthen the model or it may lead to restructuring the model. Exceptional situations do not restructure models which are already strong, but lead to the formation of a new, more specific model. The more abstract model, however, remains a default for new situations. Most rules in such models are empirical rules, which means that they are domain sensitive and relatively easy to change when confronting information arises. Some rules, however, are less domain sensitive and are used for changing the empirical rules. Examples of such rules are pragmatic reasoning schema's. These rules too have been induced after certain experiences: experiences with causal, predictive, obligatory or permitting relations in it. Pragmatic reasoning schema's do not abstract from such relations because there are hardly situations in everyday life in which more abstract pragmatic reasoning schema's appear to be needed. At any rate, even if fully abstract relations are known somehow (e.g., through instruction), they seem to loose the competition with pragmatic reasoning schema's, if they would compete with them at all. Although formal reasoning schema's (e.g., the material conditional) are not induced in everyday life, they should be induced when confronted with appropriate artificial situations. Consequently, the induction framework is positive for learning possibilities of the material conditional, that is, the fully abstract logical conditional, even though such learning does not occur in everyday life.

There is no need to describe the framework and its inductive processes completely, but there are some important characteristics which have to be compared with the developmental situativity theory. Both the induction framework as well as the developmental situativity theory regard learning basically as a bottom-up, inductive process. However, they differ in the material upon which the inductive processes work. The induction framework presupposes symbolic material, whereas the developmental situativity theory presupposes non-symbolic material as elementary (although symbols are important: as tools, not as the building blocks of induction). Both theories consider top-down processes to be important elements of learning, and both recognize the instructional function of formal concepts (Holland et al. speak of technical versus folk definitions). The difference, however, lies in the nature of the concepts involved in top-down processes. The induction framework presupposes that a concept may be defined in an everyday or in a formal way, but, in contrast to the developmental situativity theory, there is no fundamental psychological difference between both ways. Although these differences between the two theories are fundamental, the theories should not simply be opposed to each other because the developmental situativity theory may be considered to be a developmental, situated version, or even as a reframing of the induction framework. Nevertheless, the two theories do differ in hypotheses concerning Tarski's World's effectivity on the selection task, as will be seen in the next chapter. For that reason, the research that is based on the pragmatic reasoning schema theory will be reviewed.

In their search for induction of abstract inference rules, Cheng, Holyoak, Nisbett, and Oliver (1986), found that a short formal training (*Rule training*: instruction about the abstract principle of the material conditional together with some examples and tasks that may be found in introductory logic courses) was unsuccessful in facilitating logical reasoning on the selection tasks. Even a complete logic course failed to meet this objective. Besides formal instruction, concrete instruction (*Examples training*: instruction with concrete instances of the material conditional within a Wason selection task situation) in which subjects tried to solve two selection tasks after which they received feedback, was not successful either. Cheng et al. assumed that "rule training is ineffective because subjects have no ability to apply it to concrete problems and examples training is ineffective because subjects have no intuitive grasp of the rule they are being shown how to apply" (p. 305). However, a combination of the two trainings (*Rule & Examples training*) yielded a large and significant effect (61 percent correct against 25 percent in the control group). Subjects only seem to be able to reason according to formal logic when the rule is taught explicitly along with the way to apply it in a specific situation.

Although the results of the Cheng et al. experiment are interesting, the Rule & Examples training is not a very persuasive means to facilitate inductive processes. Subjects receive all ingredients to solve a problem that is no more than a near-transfer task of the training tasks. More persuasive is a long term formal training (e.g., three or four years instruction in statistics, mathematics, linguistics, computer science, Lehman & Nisbett, 1990) which does induce formal logical rules as measured with Wason selection tasks as far transfer tasks. The results of this study are important as, since the critique of Thorndike (Lehman and Nisbett recall), formal education was considered to be incapable of generating such induction. Despite this success, the outcomes of formal education are not very impressive when the efficiency of instruction is taken into account. The remainder of this thesis is dedicated to the question whether instruction using Tarski's World, will be able to efficiently facilitate far transfer reasoning on the selection task.

PART II

Instruction in Logic

4

Tarski's World: Computer-Based Instruction in First-order Predicate Logic[1]

4.1 The Importance of Logic Instruction

Logic instruction is an interesting subject within instructional as well as psychological perspectives. The psychological interest in logic instruction is evident from the review on human reasoning in chapter 3. The psychological perspective on logic instruction is central in this thesis, but logic instruction is interesting for instructional science too because logic is the most abstract domain available. Success in logic instruction may possibly supply principles or ideas for instruction in formal subjects in general (e.g., mathematics, linguistics, physics).

Instructional design is getting more important for logic teachers too as more students than before (think about computer scientists) are attending classes in logic and the use of logics is on the increase in the cognitive sciences. This implies that less mathematically gifted or motivated students attend logic classes too, which is an extra load on the instructional environment. Logic teachers cannot afford to have a high rate of drop-outs as cognitive scientists and computer scientists have to construct computational systems in which some type of formal logic is crucial. Especially computer scientists develop systems in which faults may cause major problems in society which can even be lethal (think about flight control systems). It would be a comfortable idea when such systems are proved to be faultless, but only few computer scientists are able to provide a proof of even small programs. Unfortunately, logic instruction often has a wrong impact on students: Some students become afraid of logic or develop a negative attitude in which logic is often considered to be useless or even illogical. Although these phenomena hardly have been studied seriously, they can easily be observed in conversations among students during breaks and many logic teachers are aware of these problems (e.g., Barwise & Etchemendy, 1990; Fung, O'Shea, Bornat, Reeves & Goldson, 1993).

Fortunately, many logic teachers have been trying to improve their lectures in some way or another. Most of these enterprises were directed to proof-theoretic assistance in the form of computer programs. Some of those programs are hardly instructive as students can only use a proof engine without any instructional feedback or help, but other programs are truly computer-assisted instruction (e.g., Suppes, 1981; Goldson, Reeves & Bornat, 1991). A very different approach can be found in Tarski's World in which proof theory is only peripheral, but in which students already learn to handle a formal language (first-order predicate logic). Instead of proof theory, the developers Barwise and Etchemendy focus on a semantical, model-theoretic view on logic and design their instruction accordingly. In the next section, Tarski's World will be described concretely before turning to its instructional significance.

4.2 The Look of Tarski's World

Tarski's World (Barwise & Etchemendy, 1990[1]) is a computer-based instruction program, named after the logician Alfred Tarski who pioneered semantics in the 30s. Tarski's World can be used in an introductory course in logic, primarily for students in the symbolic sciences like computer science, linguistics, psychology, artificial intelligence and mathematics, but as the authors indicate, it is suitable for a variety of undergraduate courses. Also, for pre-academic secondary school students this package may be a useful supplement to their mathematics classes. The goal of the instruction is that students acquire an understanding of semantic aspects of first-order logic, for example, the meaning of connectives, truth, and logical consequence. These aspects of formal logic are not easily taught by explaining them in natural language. As with learning foreign spoken languages, the best way to learn a logical language is to actually use it. Tarski's World is

---

[1] Tarski's World comes along with 'The Language of First-Order Logic', a book written by Barwise and Etchemendy. The version of Tarski's World used in this thesis is version 3.1 for the Apple Macintosh computer. Newer versions and versions for Next and Microsoft Windows are also available (for the latest information see HTTP://CSLI-WWW.STANFORD.EDU/HP/ on the Internet). For a review of the complete instruction package see Goldson & Reeves (1992; see also Hodges, 1989).

specifically designed for the purpose of facilitating learning-by-doing in an interactive graphical environment. Predicates, therefore, are interpreted instead of abstract: They refer to geometric objects and relations which can be visualized. The objects take the form of simple geometric bodies that inhabit an 8 by 8 chessboard 'world' (see Figure 4.1). Logical expressions describe so-called worlds of objects and these worlds can be visualized and altered by the student.

This is very different from most computer-based instruction in logic in which the semantical understanding is taken as self-evident while focusing directly on proof theory. When students can express themselves in a formal language and understand basic semantical aspects of logic, they can continue their logic course with Hyperproof, another computer based instruction developed by Barwise and Etchemendy (1995), which can be seen as an extension of Tarski's World which also supports proof development. In this thesis, only Tarski's World is used.

Below, Tarski's World will be described very concretely by focussing on those elements of Tarski's World students will encounter: an interpreted language, a facility for visualizing expressions, an editor, a truth-evaluator, and a game-like explanation facility.

The Interpreted Language
Tarski's World uses a First-Order Language (FOL) in which predicates have fixed interpretations, contrary to abstract predicates. FOL in Tarski's World is about three types of polyhydrons: cubes, tetrahedrons, and dodecahedrons. These objects have properties like being large or small and they are related to each other in terms of spatial positions (e.g., in front of, to the right of). The expressions a student can make are rather straightforward translations of English. A sentence like 'If d is a dodecahedron, then f has to be a cube' can be formalized in FOL by Dodec(d) $\rightarrow$ Cube(f). These translations can be placed on the screen by use of the editor of Tarski's World.

The Editor
Tarski's World has an editor for FOL which consists of the sentence window (see Figure 4.1) and the keyboard window (see Figure 4.2). A set of sentences can be saved as a file. The sentence files that accompany Tarski's World have been given names of logicians. By clicking with a mouse on the icons of the keyboard window, Tarski's World places the predicates and connectives in such a way that some necessary parentheses and spaces are being printed automatically in the sentence-window. Sentence 4 of Abelard's sentences (see Figure 4.1) was made by simply clicking on the following five buttons of the keyboard window: (1)

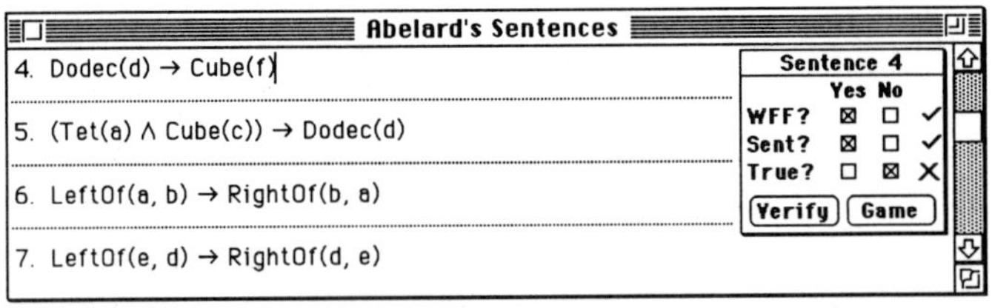

Figure 4.1. An example of a sentence window of Tarski's World.

dodec, (2) d, (3) →, (4) cube, (5) f. A student can also use the physical keyboard instead of the keyboard window, but the effort to learn the keyboard-equivalents for the FOL-symbols is likely to pay only when the student makes extensive use of the program in a short period of time.

The Worlds
The real virtue of an interpreted language lies in the possibility to visualize the FOL-expressions. The polyhydrons can be placed on a 8 by 8 grid in the world window (see Figure 4.3) simply by clicking on the icon of the object. A set of objects on the grid is called a world which can be displayed in two or three dimensions and in colors too. Worlds can be given names. The standard world files that accompany Tarski's World are named after logicians (Note that Tarski's World refers to the program, Wittgenstein's world only refers to a world file). By dragging an object around on the grid, one can move it to the desired place. Objects are removed by dragging them outside the grid. Every object can be made small, medium large or large and can be given one or more names (the alphabetic letters a - f). Objects cannot be placed on top of other objects. The spatial relations between objects, which are described in the sentence window by predicates Between, LeftOf, RightOf, FrontOf, BackOf can now be simply read

Figure 4.2. The Keyboard window of Tarski's World.

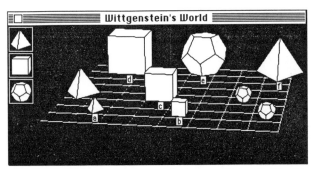

Figure 4.3. An example of a world window of Tarski's World.

out from the world window. The truth of an expression can be verified against a world. One can verify the truth of a sentence just by looking at the world to which it should refer, but when expressions get complex, it can be difficult to make a correct evaluation. Tarski's World can be asked to present feedback to a predicted truth value (see the box in the top-right corner of Figure 4.1).

The Feedback Facility
In verifying an expression, students first have to verify whether expressions are syntactically correct. Spelling and use of spaces, commas, and parentheses should be according to the rules of FOL in order to make an expression a *Well Formed Formula* ("WFF" in Figure 4.1). Tarski's World also demands that variables that are used in the expressions are bound by quantifiers. When all variables are bound by quantifiers the expression is called a *Sentence* ("Sent" in Figure 4.1). Students have to verify whether a syntactically correct expression is a Sentence or not before the truth of the expression in the current world can be verified. Students do not have to give a formal proof, but have to 'conclude' the truth of an expression intuitively. Syntax, Sentence and Truth of an expression may be verified simultaneously (assuming 'yes' for Synt, Sent, and Truth) but when the expression is syntactically wrong or if it is not a Sentence, no further evaluation will be carried out. The verification process is always performed in relation to a specific configuration of objects.

The Game
Students may encounter problems after verifying the truth of an expression: In the opinion of the student a Sentence should be true in a certain world, but Tarski's World says it is not. When disagreements of this kind occur, a student can play a game with Tarski's World. During this so-called Henkin-Hintikka

game (based on semantical tableaux) an expression will be interactively decomposed in such a way that only a single elementary statement will finally be verified against the given world. For short expressions truth-tables would be suitable, but while expressions are growing more complex, the playing of the Game is much nicer.

A notion of how the Game works will be gained by presenting an example of an exercise of 'The Language of First-Order Logic'. In the first exercise about the material (bi)conditionals (if - then statements) the student has to evaluate a number of conditional expressions (Abelard's sentences, see Figure 4.1) in a world called Wittgenstein's world (see Figure 4.3). The text in the book supplies truth-tables for the conditionals, and provides some English forms of conditionals. The student is told that later on in the book he or she will see that the important use of the conditional lies in conjunction with universal quantifiers. In this example the student simply has to read the expressions and evaluate them in the given world. Sentence 4 of Abelard's sentences says when d is a dodecahedron, f has to be a cube. Looking at Wittgenstein's world, it turns out that d is a cube and f is a tetrahedron. The objects of the world do not match the predicates of the conditional expression, causing some students to think that the expression is false. When verifying the conclusion that sentence 4 is not true, Tarski's World signals an X which means the conclusion was wrong. The student may understand why it is wrong after some thinking, but when the student lacks understanding he or she has the option of playing the game. After clicking on the button 'game',

(a) Tarski's World wants the student to reassure that he or she thinks the expression is false (see Figure 4.4, phase a),

(b) Tarski's World tries to convince the student that the opposite is true. In this case the expression should be true. But first Tarski's World rewrites the conditional Dodec(d) → Cube(f) into ¬Dodec(d) ∨ Cube(f) and again the student has to reassure his or her prediction (see Figure 4.4, phase b),

(c) Tarski's World chooses a part of the disjunction that is true in Wittgenstein's world, ¬Dodec(d), and asks the student again to restate his or her commitment (see Figure 4.4, phase c),

(d) Tarski's World changes the chosen statement from negative to positive, and asks the student whether he or she, negating the former prediction, agrees it must be true (see Figure 4.4, phase d),

(e) Tarski's World verifies the elementary statement against Wittgensteins world and concludes that the student has lost the game (see Figure 4.4, phase e).

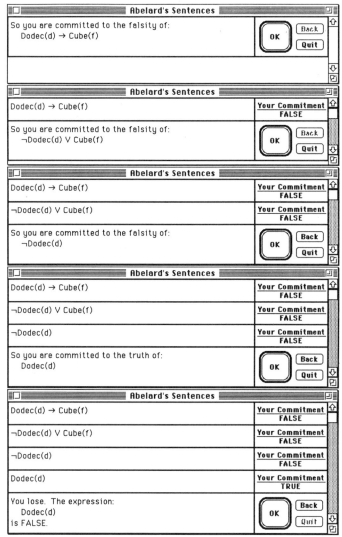

Figure 4.4. The 5 phases (from top to bottom window: phases a, b, c, d, and e) of the use of the Game for sentence 4 of Abelard's sentences (see Figure 4.1) as verified in Wittgenstein's world (see Figure 4.3).

Of course, most students will see their mistake at step b, after which they can quit the game. The more complex an expression is, the more profitable the Game-playing will be when the student does not understand a truth evaluation. However, even in simple expressions students can overlook some facts-of-the-world or misread an expression. In those cases the Game can be enlightening

Table 1
Rules of the Game of Tarski's World for the various forms of statements

Form	Students commitment	
	True	False
P ∧ Q	student has to choose one of P, Q that is true	Tarski's World has to choose one of P, Q that is true
P ∨ Q	Tarski's World has to choose one of P, Q that is false	student has to choose one of P, Q that is false
∃x P(x)	student has to choose an object that satisfies P(x)	Tarski's World has to choose an object that satisfies P(x)
∀x P(x)	Tarski's World has to choose an object that does not satisfy P(x)	student has to choose an object that does not satisfy P(x)
¬P	replace ¬P by P and switch commitment	replace ¬P by P and switch commitment
P → Q	replace P → Q by ¬P ∨ Q	replace P → Q by ¬P ∨ Q
P ↔ Q	replace P ↔ Q by (P → Q) ∧ (Q → P)	replace P ↔ Q by (P → Q) ∧ (Q → P)

too. In this example only a few rules are utilized. The rule that will be used depends on the students commitment and the form of the expression. In the example above only Tarski's World had to make choices in decomposing the expression. In other situations the student has to make choices. See Table 4.1 for an overview of all rules of the Game.

A weak point of the Game is that it may lead to a conclusion that is correct considering the game itself, but which does not refer to the truth-value of the initial expression. This only happens when a student makes a wrong choice during one of the steps. Students should be made aware of this possible side effect of the Game, as 'The Language of First-Order Logic' indeed does.

4.3 The Significance of Tarski's World

In this section it will be argued that Tarski's World facilitates situated action within the instructional domain. But first, the ideas and intentions of the developers of Tarski's World will be discussed briefly. Greeno (1990) reviews Tarski's World as an interesting example of explorative instruction which is also related to situated action. The relation is obvious when realizing that the developers of Tarski's World have been working on a special type of model-theoretic semantics, called *situation semantics* (Barwise & Perry, 1983; for an introduction see Barwise & Etchemendy, 1989) which has a much greater psychological plausibility than other semantics because the situations to model are allowed to be inconsistent to each other and the extensions may be partial. Also, context matters as situation semantics holds that truth values cannot be assigned to isolated sentences. Situation semantics has been recognized as an early situativity theory (Greeno & Moore, 1993) and several aspects —as the ones just mentioned— are indeed in line with the developmental situativity theory. However, I understand situation semantics as a theory in which the nature of the relation between symbol systems and reality is fixed (although within this fixed relation it is more flexible than other model-theoretic accounts such as possible worlds semantics which inspired Johnson-Laird to construct his mental model theory). A fixed relation does not commensurate with the developmental situativity theory in which the relation between representation and reality is assumed to be dynamic.

The developers of Tarski's World have not only been reforming model-theory in logic, they have also proposed a radical change in proof theory. In logic, graphics or diagrams have always been used as heuristics for finding the real proof apart from the evident illustrative, didactic purposes. Barwise and Etchemendy (1991), argue that this is too restrictive. Logic should not only be a formalization of verbal thinking, but also of visual thinking because some visual representations can form a powerful, simple step in a proof, while such a step may be very difficult and elaborate to represent linguistically. Barwise and Etchemendy refer to Kosslyn (1980) who shows that for some tasks visual information processing is more efficient than propositional processing. Therefore, they are working on a formal logic that allows multiple forms of representation to be part of proofs (*heterogeneous proof*).

Although Tarski's World and Hyperproof are clearly and primarily meant to be instructional tools for an introduction in standard first-order logic, it is unlikely that both packages would have been developed without situation semantics theory at the background. Also, Hyperproof may be considered as a reformal of first-order logic to a heterogeneous proofs logic (based on natural deduction methods) for instructional purposes. Regardless of the intentions and theories of the developers, Tarski's World has attracted logic teachers and educational researchers for several reasons: Tarski's World has been expected to be helpful in lowering a threshold of fear of formal systems (Fung et al., 1993) and the use of interactive graphics has been expected to facilitate problem solving behavior in an explorative way (Greeno, 1990) which also supports *situativity-in-domain* (SiD). While the developmental situativity theory assumes that any action or thinking within instruction is situated, SiD means that the activity is directed towards the subject matter.

Instruction usually does not invite students to be situative within the subject matter itself. Instead, students' situativity is, for example, directed towards strategies for credits which is quite different from learning and understanding subject matter. The term *SiD instruction* will be used for the type of instruction that strongly facilitates situativity towards or within the subject matter. Therefore, a description of the factors determining the facilitative nature of Tarski's World for situativity-in-logic will be given.

Situativity-in-Domain in Tarski's World

The domain of geometry as used in Tarski's World is more than just an exemplification of a formal logic, it is a micro-world in which most semantical aspects of first-order logic are actually learned. As this micro-world is assumed to be a situated learning environment, two interpretations of situativity have to be ruled out.

The first of these interpretations is to conflate situativity with concreteness. Although concreteness is an important aspect of situativity, it does not define situativity alone as concreteness of subject matter does not by itself lead to understanding. One can easily design instruction for logic in which geometry is used to provide concrete examples without the slightest possibility of SiD. For example, Tarski's World without the feedback facility and with only given worlds, would constitute a concrete context for learning to use a first-order language, but it would not support SiD. For SiD, activity with concrete objects (being instantiations of everyday concepts) is needed while feedback should be experienced in relation to that activity.

The second interpretation concerns the conflation of situativity with authenticity, which is popular in instructional science. Tarski's World does not provide for authentic logical tasks. Proofs do not go beyond the intuitive (one can 'see' whether an expression is true or not in a 'world') or the explanatory (as in the Game). Students are not asked to provide formal proofs and consequently, the tasks that can be done using Tarski's World are not authentic. If it is not for its concreteness or authenticity, what makes Tarski's World suitable for situativity-in-logic? Tarski's World is assumed to facilitate situativity due to its specific interactive graphical representation, its use of natural language concerning concepts with everyday-like meanings and its feedback facility. Through these three aspects a micro-world is created to which a student can adapt. Once a micro-world is adapted to, it becomes an *artificial psychological reality* for the student.

An important aspect of an interactive graphical representation is that it allows for direct manipulation (e.g., Norman, 1986) which means that between the representation to be manipulated and the student there is not a layer of symbols (as in old command-line operating systems), but merely a tool (e.g., a mouse). As a consequence of direct manipulation, the geometric representations in the world window of Tarski's World are no longer considered to be representations but instead as objects on their own, meaning that they refer neither to objects in the real world nor to mathematical concepts. As there are only few objects in this artificial world and the only statements that matter concern spatial relations, it is a world to which students easily adapt. Therefore, the world window is an artificial psychological reality in which thinking and acting function on the level of simple, everyday concepts: situativity.

Tarski's World's FOL can be used to formalize statements in natural language as far as they concern spatial relations about the three types of polyhedrons of the world window. In combination with a world, the statements are about everyday concepts and for that matter they can be processed fully in a situated mode. Most statements in natural language are evidently true or false in a specific world, but students may be unsure about the logical truth value of other statements. The feedback and Game facilities of Tarski's World can be seen as simulations of the feedback and explanations logic teachers may provide.

As said before, the combination of the interactive graphical representation, the natural language behind the expressions and the feedback facility allow for SiD of students. However, instruction facilitating only SiD would not be very powerful as students would not have the necessary tools to be able to work on a more abstract level than the level of everyday concepts. But Tarski's World also has a formal component (the logical formula editor) and only by using this component can a student use the feedback and Game facilities. Therefore, situative and formal aspects are combined in a tangled way in Tarski's World. In the next section, these aspects will be unraveled in such a way that approximations of an only-SiD version and an only-formal version of Tarski's World appear. With these versions of Tarski's World, it will be able to demonstrate experimentally the advantage of a combined SiD and formal instruction over only-SiD or only-formal instruction.

4.4 Tarski's World in an Experimental Environment

In order to learn about semantics in logic, it is crucial to experience the differences between meanings in the situativity with natural language and geometric objects on the one hand and meanings in the formal language on the other hand. Due to the feedback of Tarski's World a comparison of the two meanings is possible. As the meaning of the formal language is considered to be the correct one in Tarski's World, students who use deviating semantics are forced to change these. As the logical meaning is imposed on students, they may, without understanding, adapt to logic on test items which are similar to the training tasks (within the same context the conditionals have different content). Those test-tasks are called near-transfer tasks. However, when logic is adapted to in test items which are quite different from training tasks (far-transfer tasks: both context as well as content of the conditional are different), the student is assumed to understand the use of logic. The learning process leading to far transfer is in line with the notion of induction as proposed by Holland, Holyoak, Nisbett, and Thagard (1986).

As the material conditional has proved to be hard to learn using the Wason selection task as a criterion (see chapter 3) and as Tarski's World is an environment in which confronting meanings concerning conditionals can compete with each other, it is obvious to test the instructional effectivity of Tarski's World using the selection task as far-transfer task. As it is expected that only the combination of SiD and formal aspects of Tarski's World is effective, only-SiD and only-formal versions of Tarski's World have been developed. In this section, these versions and their theoretical implications are described, along with the instruction that will be used in the experiments. It should be noted that during the period of experimentation several small parts of the instruction and its environment have been changed. The description below refers to the final instruction as used in the last experiment (see chapter 7). Some parts of the instruction used in the earlier experiments are now considered to be irrelevant or misleading and some parts of the latest material were not used in the earlier experiments. The changes in instructional material will be described in chapters 5, 6 and 7.

Experimental Impairment of Tarski's World

In order to demonstrate experimentally that a combined SiD and formal instruction is superior to only-SiD instruction or only-formal instruction, two versions of Tarski's World have been developed: TW^{SiD}, an only-SiD version of Tarski's World and TW^F, an only-formal version of Tarski's World. Tarski's World itself will be abbreviated as TW.

In TW^{SiD} the logical formulas are no longer displayed, instead, students use the equivalent of the logical expression: its translation in natural language. Tasks for TW may consist of construction of a world and a logical expression, whereas in TW^{SiD} only construction of a world is needed. The feedback facility remains operative, as an invisible logical equivalence of the natural expression is the factual expression upon which the proof is based. To the student, it looks as if the truth of a natural sentence can be verified in a specific world. Most expressions used in this experiment have a rather simple content. They concern spatial relations of three types of polyhedrons which can appear in three sizes. Natural sentences with such physical content are situated (in a world). This version of Tarski's World is as situative as it can be with the possibility of experimental comparison to TW and TW^F. However, the natural sentences in TW^{SiD} may not always be processed as directly as usual in situated action because they were not allowed to be ambiguous and consequently some of the expressions are rather artificial. But within the experiment, this version is clearly much more SiD-facilitative than the formal version of Tarski's World.

The key feature of TW^F is the absence of visualized worlds. In this version students have to translate the natural sentences into logic. They also have to verify the truth, but in TW^F this is merely a check whether their translations are semantically wrong. Students know that a correct verification is necessary, but not sufficient for a good translation. TW^F is a purely formal instruction because it is unimportant whether the expression is about abstract symbols like A, B and C or more concrete symbols like Cube, Small and Between. Although the student may try to visualize a sentence by imagining a situation with, for example, a small cube standing between two objects, such a model will not be helpful when the student is not able to verify the sentence in it.

TW^{SiD} gives all opportunity to induction according to the induction framework (Holland et al., 1986). Although students receive feedback based on their own worlds, it is especially the feedback based on the given worlds (see below) that confronts students with the logical rules of the if - then statements as opposed to the pragmatic rules of natural if - then expressions. This provides students with the space for discovering the logical rules, a space that students using TW^F lack. However, TW^{SiD} subjects have no means or tools other than natural language to abstract from it. It will be very difficult to detach and restructure the pragmatic meaning from the natural sentence without formal tools. Therefore, induction in such an only-SiD environment may need much more confrontations than can be provided. Some near transfer may be expected from this instruction, but the far transfer needed for solving the Wason selection tasks will not be reached. This now, may be accomplished through instruction in TW. Students using TW have access to the same feedback that is available in the TW^{SiD}-instruction, but they also have to translate natural sentences into formal expressions and by doing so, they use the formal language as a tool in finding the correct solution and, perhaps less consciously, adapting to the logical meaning of the conditional. The formal language is basically a tool for restructuring meaning. It is expected that working with formal tools in a situative environment clears the path to induction beyond the near-transfer level. Therefore, TW instruction is expected to facilitate logical reasoning more on the selection tasks than the other two instructions which will not go much further than a control group baseline. In my reading of the induction framework, Holland et al. would not predict a difference between TW- and TW^{SiD}-instructions as one of the two —equivalent— representations is redundant.

Instructional Design for the Material Conditional

All experiments in this thesis concern the material conditional. Although this is an elementary connective, instruction must be very carefully designed in order to be effective. At any rate, effectivity should not be low as a result of students' inexperience with Tarski's World as an instructional environment. Therefore, considerable effort should be made in introducing the subjects to the environment itself: the *general training*. This training will be presented in all experiments to every subject in any condition. Two small tasks will conclude the general training in order to test the subjects' skill in using basic Tarski's World operations. The experimental *instructional treatment* will be based on a number of conditional statements concerning polyhedrons. All experimental groups will have to use the same statements, but the precise tasks differ between the groups. The *test* will have near-transfer and far-transfer items. The near-transfer items will be constructed in the Tarski's World environment. The far-transfer items will be Wason selection tasks and will be used to pretest and to posttest subjects. The design of the general training, the instructional treatment, and the test will be outlined below. Some instructional material is included in the appendix.

General Training
The general training prepares subjects for the instructional treatment and therefore, all aspects of the treatment, except the material conditional, should be made known to them. The general training consist of an introduction, several demonstrations, several tasks, and finally a test. Each of these will be described briefly.

A short introduction on first-order logic and Tarski's World is provided by a text in which basic logical concepts (e.g., variables, predicates, quantifiers, truth) are described and in which the subjects become acquainted with elements of Tarski's World. This text is followed by demonstrating Tarski's World.

During the demonstrations all basic activities which are needed to use Tarski's World are presented in text and demonstrations. There are three series of demonstrations: (a) demonstrations of construction and change of particular worlds in the world window (e.g., to give an object a different name), (b) demonstrations concerning the logical formula editor (e.g, correcting a sentence), and (c) demonstrations concerning the feedback and the Game facilities (e.g., to verify the truth of a sentence). After each series, the subjects are given the opportunity to use Tarski's World themselves. After the demonstrations and the try-out sessions subjects roughly know how to use Tarski's World.

Once a student is able to control the user-interface, several tasks are presented in order to train the subjects further in: (a) the use and construction of specific worlds (two tasks), (b) translation of natural sentences into logical expressions using quantifiers (All: $\forall$, Some: $\exists$), connectives (And: $\wedge$, Or: $\vee$, Not: $\neg$) and the predicates of Tarski's World (eight tasks), and (c) verifying sentences on syntax and truth (two tasks).

This training is considered to be a sufficient preparation for the instructional treatment, but some tasks have been added in order to prepare subjects to the test (see below). In the test all subjects will have to do tasks which are different from the tasks during the treatment. For that reason, two tasks were added to the general training to acquaint subjects with some syntactic and notational aspects of the material conditonal and to provide them with some examples of conditional expressions in logic. Also, some additional tasks were provided in which hidden worlds or hidden sentences are used in order to familiarize subjects with similar tasks used during the test as they may not receive such tasks during the treatment,

The general training concludes with a test in order to determine subjects ability to work with Tarski's World. One item addresses the ability to construct a world. Another item addresses the skill to express oneself in logic.

Instructional Treatment

The treatment contains of 18 sentences grouped together in six problems focusing on the material conditional (see Appendix, Table A.1). The sentences confront students with aspects of the logical conditional which are not common in everyday life conditionals. Most students will find a "If P then Q" statement only sensible in situations "P and Q" and "P and NOT-Q". In the first situation the statement is true, in the second it is false. In logic however, the statement is also true in situations "NOT-P and Q" and "NOT-P and NOT-Q". It is assumed that situated activity in such situations may alter students concept of conditional expressions. Instruction consists of several conditional expressions. The given worlds in which the expressions may be verified, agree with "P and NOT-Q" situations, "NOT-P and Q" situations, and "NOT-P and NOT-Q" situations. "P and Q" situations are not presented, because in most tasks subjects are expected to build such situations by themselves. The experience that conditional statements are true in many more situations than one is normally aware of, is thought to be of importance for developing a falsifying stategy (modus tollens) in the Wason selection task. During the treatment, the modus tollens is neither described nor demonstrated because induction of the modus tollens must be attributed to the largest possible extent to the experiences of the student (the use of formal explanations during the instructional treatment supplies the treatment with an unwanted top-down element).

What subjects have to do with these expressions depends on the condition to which they are allocated. Subjects in the SiD-condition (receiving the TW^{SiD}-instruction) have to construct a world in each problem so that the sentences of the problem are true (or false in some tasks) and they have to verify the truth of the natural sentences in an available second world too. Subjects in the formal condition (receiving the TW^F-instruction) have to translate the sentences in Tarski's World FOL. They too have to verify the truth in the same world available to the TW^{SiD}-group, but to the TW^F-group this is only a check on the correctness of the translation as they cannot see the world. Subjects in the SiD as well as formal condition (SiD&F; receiving the TW-instruction) have to do both: construct a world and make a translation (see Appendix Figure A.5 and Table A.2 for an example of a task for the three conditions).

Test

The test for logical conditional reasoning has two seperate parts: a far-transfer test containing four Wason selection tasks as items and a near-transfer test containing three Tarski's World tasks as items. Below, both tests are described.

All four Wason selection tasks of the far-transfer test have arbitrary content, meaning that the conditional rules are not familiar to the subjects. Arbitrary tasks may be concrete, and yet not familiar. Two tasks are rather abstract (Cards and Blocks; see Appendix, Figures A.6 and A.7) and two are concrete (Jars and Birds; see Appendix, Figures A.8 and A.9). It is often found that concrete tasks are easier than abstract tasks. In this study, however, it is the improvement within a task that matters, not the differences between tasks. Only when tasks show very different patterns, individual results will be reported.

The Wason selection tasks will be scored in three measures which are not independent of each other but have different interpretations. The first is the *number of correct tasks* (NC: Number of Correct items) reflecting the consistency of correct choices during the test. The second measure is derived by dichotomizing NC (0 till 3 = 0, 4 = 1) after which the group *percentage correct on all tasks* (PAC: Percentage All items Correct) can be calculated. PAC reflects the amount of stable and correct responses during the test within a group. PAC is less informative but theoretically stronger than NC. Therefore, NC will be reported only when PAC is indiscriminative or when trends in both measures are dissimilar. The third measure is the *logic index* (Pollard & Evans, 1987), which indicates the number of falsifying selections (P or NOT-Q, when the rule has the form of "If P then Q") relative to not-falsifying selections (NOT-P or Q). The logic index specifically scores +1 for a P or NOT-Q selection and -1 for a NOT-P or a Q selection. This produces a 5-point scale from -2 to 2. The logic index can be seen as the extent to which the choices agree with logical choices, but as Pollard and Evans point out, it does not measure any personal logical ability, strategy or insight. The logic index is the most sensitive of the three measures and particularly useful for its potential to measure a change in response other than incorrect - correct. For instance, the improvement of a NOT-P and Q choice to a P choice is considerable (3 points on the 5-point scale), but PAC and NC are insensitive to it.

As a near-transfer test, one new task out of each instruction type (TW, TW^{SiD}, and TW^F; see Appendix, Table A.3) is constructed. All subjects in the experimental groups have to make these test items. The item with task characteristics similar to the instruction type is considered to be the nearest transfer task. The other tasks (which are to be presented counterbalanced before presentation of the 'nearest transfer task' of each condition) are near-transfer tasks too, although farther transfer will be needed. It should be noted that the SiD&F- and SiD-items in the near-transfer test contain very unusual sentences in logic as well as in natural language. The form is "There is something for which it holds that if it is an A, statement B is true". Many students interpret such a sentence as "If there is an A, statement B is true". Although artificial, it is thought to be a good test sentence as sentences of the latter type are too easy (and therefore indiscriminative between conditions) to translate or to predict the truth-value after the treatment.

The near-transfer test will be analyzed by using *percentages correct* on each item. For each verification, subjects have to fill in the degree of certainty about their expected truth value (uncertain, more or less certain, certain). A task is considered to be solved only when the student is not uncertain about his or her conclusion given a correct translation and an agreeable world. Besides errors related to the material conditional, subjects can make other errors too in the items TW and TW^F (e.g., syntactic errors or errors concerning quantification). Therefore, the percentages correct may be misleading. The near-transfer test will be scored also on the number of items with *conditional errors* only (a 4-point scale variable). This score is more subject to the interpretation of the rater, but the interrater reliability is high (93 percent). For the types of errors involved see Appendix, Table A.4.

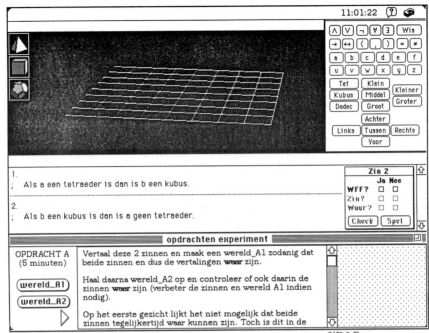

Figure 4.5. The first task of the instructional treatment in the TW$^{\text{SiD\&F}}$-condition.

Implementation of the Research Version of Tarski's World

For the experimental requirements as described above, Tarski's World had to be modified. For that purpose, the source-code of Tarski's World version 3.1 for Apple Macintosh was made available by the developers Barwise and Etchemendy. The modified program has been embedded in an instructional shell.

The shell, written in Hypercard 2.1, provided for all text, explanation, tasks, and tests used in the experiment. The shell also controlled Tarski's World: It automatically opens and quits the program; it opens, saves and closes files when the subject starts or finishes a task; it switches between 2D and 3D world representation. The shell also provides for a help function that presents information about every screen element (including Tarski's World). The shell also launched the demonstrations.

Demonstrations of basic Tarski's World operations, e.g., changing the size of an object, were made by recording the procedures with ScreenRecorder and the editing of the recordings by MediaTracks. Recorded mouse clicks were added to the demonstrations to make them sound real too. During a series of

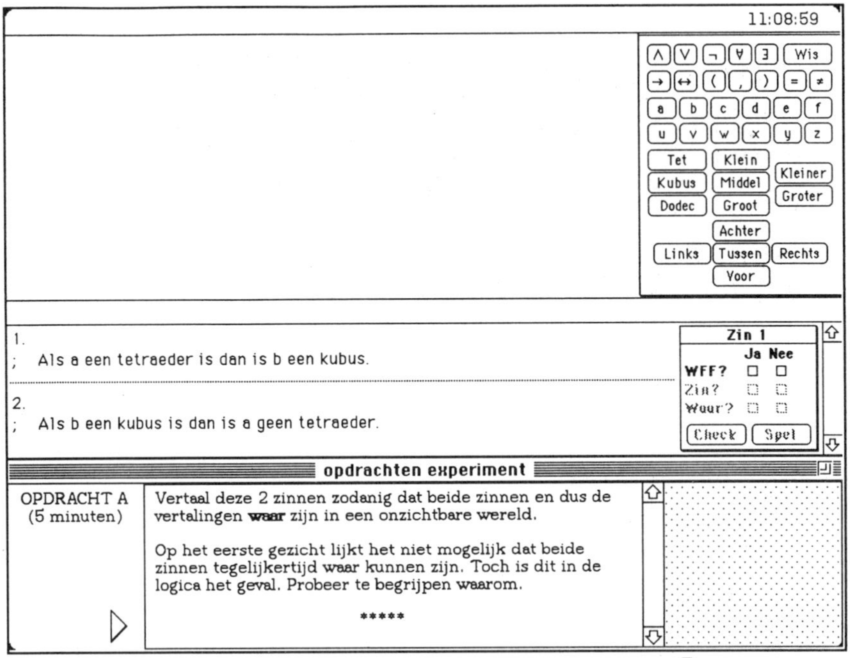

Figure 4.6. The first task of the instructional treatment in the TW^F-condition.

demonstrations, subjects can return to any part of the series, but after quitting, a subject can not see them again. However, the Help function or personal help should be sufficient to assist the subject later on.

Several small aspects have been modified in Tarski's World to facilitate communication with the instructional shell and to meet experimental requirements. The menu bar was removed to ensure that Tarski's World would be controlled solely by the shell and because only some of the options in Tarski's Worlds menu bar are useful for the experiments. All text of the user-interface of Tarski's World has been translated to Dutch in order to rule out possible differences between subjects in their apprehension of English. Even though the use of language in Tarski's World is not really a problem for most Dutch undergraduates, the use of two languages would stress the difference between the shell and Tarski's World. It has been tried to design the experimental environment as a whole. For that reason, the shell window never overlaps Tarski's World windows and vice versa (all windows have fixed positions on the screen). See Figure 4.5 for an illustration of TW. When verifying the truth of an expression (true or false) during the near-transfer test, a subject will be asked how certain he or she is about the truth (very certain, moderately certain, uncertain).

TW^F (see Figure 4.6 for an ilustration) has been created by removing the world window. Although there is a world in which the subjects can evaluate their expressions, this world is not visible. TW^{SiD} (see Figure 4.7 for an illustration)

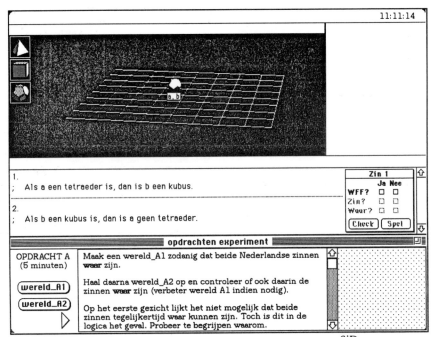

Figure 4.7. The first task of the instructional treatment in the TW^{SiD}-condition.

was created by removing the keyboard window and by changing the color of the logical expressions (black) of the sentence window to the color of the background (white). The equivalents of the logical expressions in natural language remained visible. During the instructional treatment, the Game has to be disabled because it cannot be used in the TW^{SiD} and TW^F versions of Tarski's World: The Game uses the logical expression as well as the world.

Data will be logged in two files during the Test and the instructional treatment: TW-data file and General-data file. The TW-data file will be used for logging the complete situation of every evaluation the subject makes: the world configuration (all blocks are described by form, size, and position), the logical expression, and the evaluation the subject asked for (concerning Synt, Sent, and Truth and the response of Tarski's World). The General-data file (nearly SPSS format) will be used for logging personal data about the subject, the date of the experiment, condition, time data concerning the treatment and the test, data of the far-transfer test, and data of a questionaire (for some experiments).

PART III
Research with Tarski's World

5

Situativity versus Formality in Logic Instruction Part 1

5.1 Introduction

In this chapter, the first two experiments with Tarski's World are described. The question that drives this research is whether a combined SiD and formal instruction is more effective than one-sided instruction (SiD or formal) concerning learning to reason logically. Tarski's World has all features to be optimistic about its effectivity. Tarski's World has been developed particularly to teach students semantical aspects of logic amongst which the meaning of the material conditional (see chapter 4). As far as I know, this is the only instructional environment in formal logic in which semantical goals are central.

The program is clearly in line with the induction framework (see chapter 3), in which learning depends on experiencing new 'rules' which may compete with available old ones. However, the induction framework does not predict a large difference between the only-SiD (TW^{SiD}) and the SiD&F (TW) instruction as the languages (natural language and formal language) used within the instructional treatment are equivalent (see section 4.3 for explanation of abbreviations). It is the feedback on the expectations of students which matters for induction.

Tarski's World is also agreeable with the developmental situativity theory (see chapter 2), but in contrast to the induction framework, the developmental situativity theory predicts a difference between TW^{SiD} and TW in effectivity. TW^{SiD}, only facilitating SiD, will not easily lead to an abstract use of the material conditional, which is needed for the Wason selection task. Generalizations may be reached on the same, fully situated level and within a not too different context. TW^{SiD}, therefore, may be effective on near-transfer tasks. TW-instruction provides for a formal language that is used as a tool to detach meaning more easily from the used predicates and connectives.

Theoretically (according to the induction framework as well as the developmental situativity theory), the only-formal instruction (TW^F) is considered to be ineffective because the feedback provided by this instruction can only tell whether an expression is translated incorrectly into FOL. The student is not informed about the situation in the World to which the expression refers. As this reduction of semantical evaluation (feedback) is severe, TW^F functions as a control condition. But, TW^F should not be equated to formal instruction in logic because no explicit information will be provided about the material conditional neither before nor during the treatment. Although TW^F, if added with a formal text (comprising of definitions, several representations, and examples of the material conditional) is not expected to be more effective as TW^F alone, such a text may be effective in combination with TW and, to a lesser extent, with TW^{SiD} and consequently, it may blur the effects of the instructional treatment. Therefore, no explanatory text about the material conditional will be added.

For the far-transfer test, it is hypothesized that TW is more effective than TW^{SiD} and TW^F. Only two selection tasks are used for these experiments. For the near-transfer test it is hypothesized that for each sort of instruction the best result will be on the testitem with task characteristics similar to the instruction type: the nearest transfer task. Furthermore, TW^{SiD}-instruction will lead to better outcomes than the TW^F-instruction, although the effect may be small for the SiD&F and the F-items due to lack of experience of the SiD-group with expressing conditional statements into logic. TW-instruction will have better outcomes on all items than the other instructions.

5.2 The Pilot Experiment

Method

Subjects
30 technical students (24 male, 6 female; mean age 21.6 years, $SD = 1.9$) who were enrolled in an introductory logic course at the University of Twente volunteered for the experiment. They were paid a small fee for their participa-

tion: 25 Dutch guilders (about $15). All students had reached high math-levels at secondary school and had attended several mathematics or statistics courses after secondary school. Most students had over one year full-time experience in computer programming.

Materials

A description of the materials used in this experiment can be found in section 4.4, except for the following differences: All subjects received six problems that contained altogether 20 sentences in native natural language (see Appendix, Tables A.1 and A.5, for an example of a complete task see Table A.6). Subjects could not return to a problem once a problem was completed, succesfully or not. Because the three experimental instructions differ in time-on-task inherently (which was confirmed by an unpublished usability test based on ten subjects), an additional problem was given to the SiD- and F-groups, and additional sentences were added to most problems for the SiD-group (according to the ratio between instructions in the usability test on mean time-on-sentence). The F-group had to translate 23 (20 + 3) natural sentences into first-order logic. The SiD-group was instructed to construct worlds in which 33 (20 + 3 + 10) natural sentences had to be evaluated. The TW-group (SiD&F) had to translate the 20 natural sentences into first-order logic just as the F-group and had to make a concurrent world just as the SiD-group. The additional three or thirteen sentences are redundant sentences as they do not provide qualitatively new experiences to the subjects. The Wason selection tasks used in this experiment are the Cards and the Birds tasks.

Procedure

Subjects were randomly assigned to one of three conditions: (1) SiD instruction (SiD-group), (2) formal instruction (F-group), and (3) SiD as well as formal instruction (TW-group). First, the subjects (in two groups of 15) had to make a pretest with the Wason selection tasks (about 5 minutes) in counterbalanced sequence. Then the general training was presented, which took about two hours. If they could not complete the general training's test within 8 minutes, they received additional training and personal assistance. After this test, subjects received the treatment (about 50 minutes) corresponding to the condition to which they were allocated. After instruction in conditional reasoning all subjects were given the Test (about 15 minutes). Although the experiment was self-paced, subjects were limited to four hours.

Table 5.1
Percentages correct answers on individual Wason selectiontasks and percentages correct on both items (PAC) for each condition

	Condition		
Testitem	TW n = 12	TW^{SiD} n = 11	TW^F n = 6
Cards			
pretest	0	18	17
posttest	17	18	17
Birds			
pretest	8	27	0
posttest	17	27	17
Both items			
pretest	0	0	0
posttest	17	9	17

Note. TW = Tarski's World instruction, SiD = Situativity-in-Domain, F = Formal. Attrition of 1 subject in the F condition, due to a data-logging problem during the posttest.

Results

Outcomes in percentage correct on the two individual posttest selection tasks hardly differ between groups, $\chi^2(2,29) < .50$ (see Table 5.1). Although PAC (see Table 5.1; PAC only refers to two selection tasks in this chapter) increases from 0% to 14% (McNemar binomial test, $p = .06$, one-tailed), the largest difference between conditions that would support a hypothesis, the 8% difference beteen TW- and SiD-groups on PAC, is not significant (Fisher's Exact, $p = .54$, one-tailed). All pretest - posttest differences do not reach significance levels. Although some differences between groups appear large on the pretest (18% difference on the Cards task between the TW- and S-groups, and 27% difference on the Birds task between the SiD- and F-groups), none of these differences are significant (Fisher's Exact, $p > .22$, two-tailed).

Logic indices for the selection tasks do neither differ significantly between groups nor between tests (see Tables 5.2). The logic indices hardly improve. Only the F-group increases considerably (.50) on the Birds item, but not significantly ($t(5) = 1.46$, $p = .20$, two-tailed). Other pretest - posttest differences are irrelevant (no more than .20) or even negative (the Birds tasks for the S-group).

The TW-group does not produce a better outcome on the near-transfer test than the TW^{SiD}- and TW^F-groups (see Table 5.3). On the contrary, the TW-group has the highest error rate ($F(2,24) = 5.66$, $p < 01$) and there is not one item on which the TW-group has the highest percentage correct. Instead,

Table 5.2
Logic indices on individual Wason selectiontasks for each condition

	Condition					
	TW		TWSiD		TWF	
Testitem	n = 12		n = 11		n = 6	
	M	(SD)	M	(SD)	M	(SD)
Cards						
pretest	.75	(.45)	.82	(1.08)	1.00	(.63)
posttest	.92	(.67)	1.00	(.77)	1.00	(.63)
Birds						
pretest	.83	(.58)	1.09	(.83)	.17	(1.33)
posttest	.83	(.83)	.73	(1.19)	.67	(1.03)
Both items						
pretest	.79	(.40)	.95	(.65)	.58	(.92)
posttest	.88	(.64)	.86	(.87)	.83	(.75)

Note. TW = Tarski's World instruction, SiD = Situativity-in-Domain, F = Formal. Attrition of 1 subject in the F condition, due to a data-logging problem during the posttest.

TW-subjects scored lowest on two of the three items. Differences between groups are considerable for the SiD- and F-items ($\chi^2(2,29) = 6.50$, $p < .05$, for the SiD-item and $\chi^2(2,29) = 8.45$, $p < .05$ for the F-item) in favor of the TWSiD-group. Groups do not differ significantly on SiD&F-item, $\chi^2(2,29) = 1.87$.

Discussion

The results do not support the theory as differences between conditions are low, and often contrary to the expectations. However, as the effect of Tarski's World instruction is rather low on the far-transfer test (even for the most successful group), important differences between conditions would be difficult to obtain anyway. There may be several factors causing ineffective instruction. These factors can be grouped into instructional-design factors or into instructional implementation and methodological factors. There are obvious flaws in instructional design for this experiment, but these were intended in order to have comparable conditions and to be able to interpret the results to the largest extent as effects of experiences during the treatment. Before strengthening instruction, it is important to find and eliminate implementation and methodological problems.

In this experiment, the most likely factor disturbing positive learning effects is the time available for the whole session. Although subjects were highly motivated and worked hard (according to the impression of the experimenters),

Table 5.3
Percentages correct solutions and the number of conditional errors on the near-transfer test for each condition

	Condition		
Dependent variables	TW n = 11 - 12	TW^{SiD} n = 10 - 11	TW^F n = 6 - 7
% correct			
SiD&F-item	67	50	83
SiD-item	9	55	14
F-item	33	91	71
Conditional errors: M (SD)	1.91 (.70)	.70 (.82)	1.50 (1.05)

Note. TW = Tarski's World, SiD = situativity-in-domain, F = formal.

many subjects were not able to complete the treatment. Those subjects who had not yet finished the treatment, were asked to start working on the test after 225 minutes.[1] These students may have been more fatigued and demotivated (by time pressure) than other students. This would not be very troublesome if the sample was very large and all conditions had the same amount of slow students. Unfortunately, the sample is very small and especially the subjects in the TW-condition spend more time on the treatment than subjects in the two other conditions ($F(2,26) = 12.19$, $p < .001$). Consequently, more TW-subjects than other subjects did not complete the treatment. The TW-group needed 58 percent more time for the treatment (63 minutes against 38 minutes for the SiD-group, and 42 minutes for the F group). The difference would even have been larger when slow subjects would not have been forced to end the treatment. The procedure to control for time-on-task clearly failed to succeed. Nevertheless, the results do not show an effect of time-on-task at all, as would be expected (the more time-on-task, the better results). The results on the far-transfer test reveal no difference between groups, and the outcomes for the near-transfer test are, globally, the best for the group with the lowest treatment time, the TW^{SiD}-group. An interpretation of these results requires a closer look at the time-on-task literature (for a review see Anderson, 1981).

Time-on-task is defined as the time spent on tasks in relation to the total instruction time (which may include any activities of the student, e.g., daydreaming). Although a higher time-on-task implies that the student —as a side effect of the instructional manipulation— has worked longer too, a longer

---

[1] Precise data about the treatment is not available as the logging procedure for the TW-data file (see chapter 4) only worked during the near-transfer test (only notations of the experimenter are available, but these may not be very reliable).

time-on-task cannot be simply equated to a longer instruction time. Research on time-on-task has been driven to keep students working in order to make a period of time more efficient. The period of time in research on time-on-task (often a series of lessons during several months) is much longer than the one-hour instruction in conditional reasoning of this experiment. It is not certain that the results of time-on-task research generalize to such a short period. Another point is that most students enjoy working with Tarski's World and they get feedback as soon as they need it. This makes Tarski's World a very stimulating and motivating environment. The time-on-task, therefore, is nearly identical to the instruction time. That is, when a task is defined as a complete problem within the instructional treatment. Within the scope of most instructional research, such a definition will be fine, but for more elementary, psychological research as the present study, it may be misleading. When defining time-on-task as the time spent on core-elements of a problem (understanding of the task, making decisions, evaluating the result, and reflecting the result), it is evident that time-on-task for the TW-instruction is only slightly longer than the times-on-task for TW^{SiD} and TW^F (per sentence). Most time will have to be spend on editing logical expressions and constructing worlds, which are not important activities in themselves.[2] Only in the activities of making decisions and reflecting it is expected that TW takes more time than TW^{SiD} and that TW^{SiD} takes more time than TW^F. But these extra time-on-tasks are inherent to the instructional material and are not easily compared as they are not quantitative, but qualitative in nature. The implication of this argument is that the quality and the number of feedback moments are more important than time-on-task (as well as instruction time) during the treatment.

The attempt to control 'time-on-task' by adjusting the number of expressions (based on the mean time-per-expression for each condition) failed, but whether successful or not, the control would have been inappropriate. Instead of controlling time-on-task or instruction time, the number of feedback possibilities should be controlled. Unfortunately, by using different numbers of expressions among conditions (despite the fact that these expressions were redundant), the number of feedback-possibilities differs too. As the TW- and TW^{SiD}-subjects also had to construct their own worlds, the difference in

---

[2]To speak of core elements and editing elements may be somewhat misleading as it sounds quite cognitivistic. The processes of construction of Worlds and the formulation of expressions are believed to be crucial and, e.g., it will not be possible to distinguish clearly between decision making and editing of a World as, according to the developmental situativity theory, they are intimately related. However, it can be functional to abstract from this situated level and detach core elements from editing elements in particular arguments. There is no problem in isolated abstractions, but such abstractions should not be projected backwards to the situated level.

feedback-possibilities between conditions was even larger. Subjects in the F-condition were presented 23 sentences which had to be evaluated in already available worlds (23 feedback possibilities). Subjects in the TW-condition were presented twenty sentences which had to be evaluated in the available Worlds and in self-constructed worlds (40 feedback possibilities). Subjects in the TW^{SiD}-condition were presented 33 sentences which had to be evaluated in self-constructed worlds and which could mostly be evaluated in available worlds (56 feedback possibilities). As the worlds in the TW^F-condition were invisible, feedback is not similar to the feedback that TW- and TW^{SiD}-subjects receive. It is considered to be ineffective in itself and, therefore, a second evaluation (in another invisible World) would hardly matter.

The different amount of provided feedback-possibilities and the time-limit on the treatment are favoring the TW^{SiD}-condition and, therefore, the methodology of the experiment is unsound. With these reflections in mind, most results can be explained evidently, except the high score of the F-group on the SiD&F-item of the near-transfer test. Further analysis did not reveal relevant information, likely due to the small sample and some inadequacies of a personal questionaire.[3]

Although great optimism concerning the effectivity of the TW-instruction can no longer be sustained (after all, TW-subjects spend more than an hour on the instructional treatment), the effect of time pressure should not be underestimated. The subjects already worked very intensely in the first three hours (students were hardly interested in a coffee break!). They might not even have noticed that they were getting tired. When the difficult part, the instructional treatment, is presented, students may have easily been demotivated when realizing that they were running out of time and when they saw other subjects already leaving the room. It is not unlikely that they did not give the selection tasks a real second thought (although the predicates of the rule and the order of choices were different).

There are too many flaws and mistakes in this pilot study to reach any conclusion, but many things have been learned from it. The time-on-task hypothesis does not apply to short-term instruction which is presented to very hard working students and it is theoretically incorrect within the psychological scope of this experiment. Therefore, treatment time should not be controlled, and there should be more time reserved for the treatment plus test phase of the

---

[3]Two variables of a personal questionaire, 'the number of formal courses previously attended to' (like math, statistics, etc.) and 'programming experience' are likely invalid. A number of the students misinterpreted the question about the formal courses and half of the students replied with the maximum weeks of experience in programming (99 weeks; 2 years or more full-time programming). In further experiments, instructions should be clear and programming experience might better be asked for in months.

experiment. Although the outcomes seem to be distorted by the effect of time pressure and fatigue, the effects may be smaller and the variance larger than expected. Therefore, a larger sample is needed and more personal data, e.g., concerning intelligence or reasoning skill, may be gathered in order to control for possible systematic error.

5.3 An Experiment

This experiment is a changed version of the pilot experiment in which theory and methodology are supposed to have been improved. The general training has been modified slightly, especially for reasons of time scheduling. The 20 basic sentences of the instructional treatment used in the pilot have been reduced to 19 and the additional sentences for TW^{SiD} and TW^F have been removed. The sample is twice as large and drawn from a subpopulation of first-year social science students. These students are less experienced and qualified in mathematics and computer programming than the second-year technical science students of the pilot. Therefore, they will have nearly twice as much time for the same, slightly shortened (experimental) instruction. The concrete selection task of the pilot (Birds) has been replaced by a special type of abstract selection task: Blocks (see section 4.4). The Blocks task is about relations between polyhydrons as used in Tarski's World. As subjects are familiar with situations with polyhedrons after the instructional treatment, the task becomes more concrete. Nevertheless, the rule of the task remains arbitrary. Concrete tasks are often found to be easier than abstract tasks. The effects, therefore, may be larger for the Blocks task than for the Cards task for all conditions. An intelligence test that is often regarded as a test for general reasoning skills, the Advanced Progressive Matrices (Raven, 1962), is considered to be appropriate for controlling possible systematic error.

Method

Subjects
60 social science students (39 female, 21 male; mean age 20.3 years, $SD = 4.3$) volunteered for the experiment. Educational science students (n = 35) gained study credits for their participation, while other social science students (n = 25) were paid 50 Dutch guilders (about 30 US$). Most students had reached a medium math-level at secondary school, after which they have had minor experience in mathematics or computer programming.

Materials

Materials for this experiment were the same as in the pilot except for the following changes. During the instructional treatment, subjects received six problems containing altogether 19 sentences in natural language (see section 4.4 and Appendix, Tables A.1 and A.7). As Wason selection tasks, Cards and Blocks (see section 4.4) were used. Half set of the Raven's Advanced Progressive Matrices (Raven, 1962) has been used as an intelligence test for general reasoning ability. The split-half reliability is .94 (Raven, Court & Raven, 1988).

Procedure

The procedure is similar to that of the pilot study. However, this experiment was held in two sessions of three to four hours each. In the first session all subjects had to make the pretest (the two items were presented counterbalanced; about five minutes). Then they had to do the Raven intelligence test (about 45 minutes, limit: 60 minutes), after which all subjects received the general training for about two hours. A week later, the second session took place. After some warming-up tasks subjects continued their general training for about an hour. When a subject did not complete the testitems of the general training within ten minutes, he or she received more training and personal assistance. After the skill test subjects received the instructional treatment (about 60 minutes). The near- and far-transfer tests took about twenty minutes.

Results

Differences between conditions of percentages correct on each individual selection task or on both tasks (see Tables 5.4) are not significant on both the pretest[4] and the posttest (the largest difference is the Cards task on the pretest, $\chi^2(2,59) = 3.83, p = .15$). The marginal increase on the posttest is not significant for all groups and for all tasks (McNemar binomial test, $p > .25$, one-tailed).

Logic indices (see tables 5.5) reveal a significant increase, $F(2,54) = 14.87$, $p < .001$, but the conditions do not differ in gain $F(2,54) = .71$. The gain for the TW^{SiD}- and TW^F-groups is nearly identical (difference in mean gain is .08 in favor of TW^F). The interaction of condition, testphase, and testitem is not significant, $F(1,35) = .58$. The mean increase for TW (.48) is twice as large as the gain for TW^{SiD} (.23), but not significantly larger ($F(1,35) = 1.44, p = .12$). For

---

[4]Random allocation to condition has proved sufficient as the groups do not differ in intelligence (Raven APM), or experience/level in mathematics and computer programming, $F(2,55) < 1.50$.

Table 5.4

Percentages correct on individual Wason selectiontasks and percentages correct on both items for each condition

Testitem	Condition		
	TW $n = 20$	TWSiD $n = 20$	TWF $n = 17$
Cards			
pretest	0	10	0
posttest	5	5	6
Blocks			
pretest	0	0	6
posttest	5	0	6
Both items			
pretest	0	0	0
posttest	5	0	6

Note. TW = Tarski's World, SiD = situativity-in-domain, F = formal. Attrition of 2 subjects in the F condition, due to a data-logging problem.

TW and TWSiD the gain is significantly higher for the Blocks task than for the Cards task (a difference of .50; $F(1, 38) = 5.28$, $p < .05$).

Although the F-group generally scores worst on the near-transfer test (see Table 5.6), the conditions do not differ on the number of conditional errors, $F(2,55) = .78$, on the F item, $\chi^2(2,59) = .49$, and on the SiD-item, $\chi^2(2,59) = 1.11$. A significant between-groups difference in favor of TW is only found on the SiD&F-item ($\chi^2(2,59) = 6.71$, $p < .05$). The TW-group and the F-group score highest on their nearest transfer items, though not significantly higher than the second best item (for the TW-group: McNemar test, $p = .17$, one-tailed and for the F-group, McNemar, $p = .23$, one-tailed).

Discussion

Despite the effort to improve this experiment on instructional and experimental issues, the results are not supporting. However, in this experiment nearly all trends are in the expected direction: The TW-group seems to improve more than the other groups on the selection tasks[5] and scores better on the near-transfer task. Also, TWSiD seems to score better than TWF on the near-transfer task. As these promising trends stand in stark contrast to the first experiment, it

---

[5]Although the between-group difference on the pretest is not significant, the TW group scores substantially lower than the other groups. Hence, the effect may be due to statistical regression.

Table 5.5
Logic indices on Wason selectiontasks (individual and taken together) for each condition

Testitem	Condition		
	TW n = 20 M (SD)	TW^{SiD} n = 20 M (SD)	TW^F n = 17 M (SD)
Cards			
pretest	.00 (.73)	.50 (.76)	.41 (.62)
posttest	.15 (1.04)	.60 (.60)	.76 (.56)
Blocks			
pretest	.05 (.89)	.35 (.93)	.35 (1.00)
posttest	.85 (.59)	.70 (.57)	.65 (.86)
Both items			
pretest	.03 (.70)	.43 (.61)	.38 (.57)
posttest	.50 (.65)	.65 (.49)	.71 (.64)

Note. TW = Tarski's World, SiD = situativity-in-domain, F = formal. Attrition of 2 subjects in the F condition, due to a data-logging problem.

is tempting to examine factors that possibly may have been weakening the effects. A plausible factor is the inadequacy of the instruction in relation to the characteristics of the population.

The subpopulation out of which the sample was drawn, consists of first-year social science students. As Tarski's World is believed to be suitable for all undergraduates, there should be no problem for social science students provided that they are given more time for the instruction than mathematically more experienced technical science students. Although the total instruction time seems sufficient because most subjects were able to complete the general training and the instructional treatment,[6] 30 percent of the sentences were not translated correctly by subjects in TW- and TW^F-groups (resp. 5.20 and 6.10 incorrect sentences, $t(37) = -1.00$, n.s.). This high percentage (high in respect to the simple sentences) is a serious sign that the instruction does not match the (present) capability of the subjects.

The logic indices for the far-transfer test indicate some improvement. The extent of mistakes on the selection tasks decreases significantly over all conditions, and mostly, though not significantly, for TW. This effect, that is, the withdrawal of bad reasoning habits, is not reflected by the percentages correct, which clearly reveal that subjects have not learned to reason correctly yet. This paradox

---

[6]Only 10 percent of the subjects failed to work on all 19 sentences during the treatment (no between groups differences, $F(2,56) = .22$). No subject worked on less than 15 sentences.

Table 5.6
Percentages correct solutions and the number of conditional errors on the near-transfer test for each condition

Dependent variables	Condition		
	TW n = 20	TW^{SiD} n = 20	TW^F n = 19
% correct			
SiD&F-item	50	20	16
SiD-item	30	25	16
F-item	25	35	32
Conditional errors: M (SD)	2.11 (.66)	2.05 (.60)	2.32 (.82)

Note. TW = Tarski's World, SiD = Situativity-in-Domain, F = formal.

is explained by the specific choices on the selection tasks (with rules *If P then Q*, and choices P, NOT-P, Q, and NOT-Q). On the pretest 37 percent of the subjects choose the P&Q option, while only 23 percent did so on the posttest. Only-P was chosen by 36 percent of the subjects on the pretest, but increased to 60 percent on the posttest (the P choice produces 1 point on the logic index, while the P&Q choice produces 0 points). The percentage of subjects chosing the correct option (P&NOT-Q) increases only marginally. The increase is within the expected base-rate of a repeated measure (less than five percent, e.g., Berry, 1983).

In conclusion, the present instruction is too weak for first-year social science students, which is another assault on the optimistic attitude towards Tarski's World. However, the experiment should be repeated with improved instruction in order to provide an answer of the research questions.

5.4 General Discussion

Among several options to improve instruction, three are interesting for this study: (a) additional problems in the instructional treatment for all conditions, (b) adding an explanatory text about the material conditional, and (c) using the Game facility of Tarski's World.

The option of additional problems appears attractive as it may be expected that induction would continue after its initial working (the withdrawal of mistakes) and the effects to be found can be completely interpreted in terms of experimental manipulation. But, the trend that TW leads to more improvement on the selection tasks (logic index) than the other conditions is too weak as the only basis for another experiment because it is statistically insignificant and even if it were, the trend may merely be a statistical regression (see note 5). There is a second argument against additional problems during the treatment. The six problems of the present instruction differ in complexity, but there are only a few different types of experiences. A higher complexity is unwanted and more experiences of the same type would be redundant. A negative side-effect of redundant tasks can be that students are quickly bored (as indeed a few subjects in the TW^{SiD}-condition of the pilot proclaimed) which might harm motivation. Therefore, additional problems are not a solution for the supposed weakness of instruction.

The second option is to add an explanatory text. For all conditions the text will make the subject aware of the instructional subject matter or, more specifically, its attention would be directed to invariant features of learning situations (Greeno, Moore & Smith, 1993). As Cheng et al. (1986, see chapter 3, the Rule-training) demonstrated, such instruction (a text about the abstract principles of the material conditional together with some examples and representation forms) is not effective by itself. Conform the developmental situativity theory, the formal text acts as a catalyst. However, when the text is presented within the problems, it may interfere with the working of induction and it may distort the only-SiD nature of TW^{SiD} and consequently, interpretations will not be clear. Therefore, the text should be presented only as a kind of attention generator before the instructional treatment.

The Game facility of Tarski's World is the third and most natural option to strengthen instruction. It does not disturb the situated activity (the experiences) of subjects as the Game is played only when the subjects want to. Subjects are already familiar with the Game as it can be used in the general training: They know how and when to use it. The Game reformulates conditional expressions into disjunctions and evaluates them in particular worlds. The subject is actively involved in this process (see section 4.2). This option is attractive, but the use of the Game is not without practical problems within this research. In its present state the Game cannot be used in TW^{SiD} and TW^F. The problem for TW^F is that the competitors (Tarski's World and the subject) need to be able to refer to particular polyhedrons in a particular world in order to 'prove' whether an expression is true or false. Although a special interface may be developed in which worlds are described in formal statements, such an interface would dramatically change the features of the only-formal instruction leading to a new kind of instruction which is not interesting for this study. For TW^{SiD}, the Game may be relevant, but it uses logical fomulas, and these should be avoided in an only-SiD instruction. When the user-interface of the Game is using a translator (from formal into natural language) or a database with available natural expressions, the provided explanation of the Game agrees with logic, but keeps facilitating SiD. The development of a translator or a database is very difficult and it may be a wasted effort when the Game proves to be ineffective. The effectivity of the Game should be proved before repeating the experiment in which the Game is used as an explanatory facility.

As the optimism for the first experiment turned out to be false, it is sensible to leave the central research question temporarily and to focus on the improvement of instruction. After all, Tarski's World has to be effective (i.e., at least a significant increase of correct selection tasks) before the question of the factors determining the effectivity can be addressed. Therefore, in the next experiment the effect of TW will be studied in combination with an explanatory text and the Game. The explanatory text is assumed to have the most strengthening capacity for TW. The effect of the Game is unknown,[7] but it is important to study it as it is the most natural explanation within Tarski's World. When the next experiment is successful, the central research question can be re-adressed to. A Game version for TW^{SiD} will only be developed when the effect of the Game proves to be very strong.

As the tests are not very powerful, they may need some strengthening too. However, improvement of the near-transfer test is not urgent for three reasons: (a) alternatives are not easy to construct, while there is no guarantee for improvement, (b) the near-transfer test is not very important from a theoretical point of view, and (c) the number of conditional errors seems to be useful enough for measuring a near-transfer effect. Therefore, the near-transfer test will be left unchanged. The far-transfer test, however, may easily be improved on two aspects: (a) the number of items (four instead of two items) and (b) the time-point of measurement (delayed measurement or a follow-up). A follow-up is considered to be interesting as it was noticed by the experimenters that many subjects left the training quite puzzled and that many were disappointed as the feedback of Tarski's World may still have been counterintuitive and because no feedback on the Wason selection tasks was given. A delayed far-transfer test is expected to reveal a stronger trend as the subjects may still think about the problems, perhaps even unconsciously. It is speculated, in connectionists terms, that there is continuing activity in neural networks after the treatment. Neural networks may not be able to settle down during instruction and may be easily activated long after the first session. Also, in the pilot study it was observed that a few students reached insight rather suddenly (as described by gestalt theory and potentially modelled by catastrophe or chaos theory).

---

[7]There is some indication that although the Game makes students aware of a problem, they may not be able to solve it (Van der Pal & Baars, 1994).

6

The Role of Explanation in Logic Instruction

6.1 Introduction

Tarski's World is considered to be an artificial environment in which 'real experiences' or situated action is possible but also one in which only standard logical situations occur. Theoretically (from the situated action as well as the induction framework perspective), this combination makes induction of deductive logical rules possible. In chapter five it was assumed that such instruction would be effective without any additional information (about goals or subject matter). The subjects would be able to construct the meaning of the material conditional inductively by experiencing the working of a formal system through situated action. The experiments of chapter five do not support this assumption (even when disturbing factors like time-pressure and inexperience with formal systems are taken into account). Therefore, the experiment in this chapter will focus on the strengthening of the TW-instruction.

It is assumed that subjects, receiving the instructional treatment (see section 4.4), may benefit from additional instruction that provides the gist of the matter: formalized knowledge. A formal text does not stimulate inductive processes by itself, but it may function as a catalyst when other instruction allows for such inductive processes. It is assumed that students cannot learn from formal texts without situativity.[1] Tarski's World stimulates the appropriate situativity for the domain. While working, students may compare the formalized knowledge with their experiences. The catalytic text is a top-down element in an otherwise bottom-up, inductive process.

This use of formal knowledge is different from the use of formal knowledge in formal education where it is, at most, only connected to concrete examples which rarely facilitate situativity-in-domain (SiD) and only stimulates induction on a very limited scale. Such instruction may only be effective when the given examples are similar to the test problems, as Cheng, Holyoak, Nisbett, and Oliver (1986) have demonstrated, or when students are exposed to it for a long period of time (Lehman & Nisbett, 1990). The formal text as it will be used here is not seen as the knowledge to be acquired, but merely as a tool for communication and thought. Such text may be inserted in many places within instruction but it should not interrupt students too much while working. Formal knowledge, providing an overview of the subject matter and some symbolic tools in advance of the instructional treatment, is expected to function as an attention generator and as a catalyst. This kind of tool differs from the formal language of Tarski's World in the sense that the text may be structuring a students interests before or during the learning process while the formal language may be used within the inductive process itself.

6.2 Formal Explanation in Text and Game

This experiment is set up in order to find out whether TW training (the TW-condition in the first experiment, see chapter 5) combined with formal explanation (TW+E-condition) will produce better outcomes than formal training (E-condition) alone. A third condition uses the TW+E-instruction in which the Game facility was available (TWG+E-condition). Being an extra explanatory element, the Game may influence outcomes. The effect of the E-instruction on the Wason selection tasks is expected to be low, as it is similar to the abstract rule training of Cheng et al. (1986). A larger effect is expected from the TW+E-instruction and there may be an additional effect of the Game above the effect of TW+E because it functions as a reminder of the explanatory text during the students experiences without interfering induction because students deliberately ask for this kind of explanation.[2]

---

[1] Except under certain conditions which are or should not be interesting for educational purposes (see section 8.4).
[2] Now that a formal text about the material conditional precedes the instructional treatment, instruction, notably TWG+E, is more in line with the ideas of an introductory logic course the developers of Tarski's World may have had.

Considering the study of Nisbett et al. (1990) which reveals the facilitation of long term formal education on the selection tasks, it is likely that subjects of the Cheng et al. experiment were sampled from a population that has not received formal education during a long period. The technical science and mathematics students in the present study are exposed to an intermediate amount of formal education, but they are not expected to solve the selection tasks without instruction, as the pilot study in chapter 5 indicated.

Two arbitrary Wason selection tasks are added to the conditional reasoning test as used in the previous experiment. A follow-up of the test has been added to the design. Considering the counterintuitive, sometimes astonishing experiences of the students during the treatment and the possible instant moment of understanding, it is not inconceivable that some students gain insight only days after the treatment.

Method

Subjects

55 technical science or mathematics students (49 male, 6 female; mean age 20.4 years, $SD = 1.4$) who were enrolled in an introductory logic course at the University of Twente volunteered for the experiment. They were paid a small fee for their participation: 35 guilders (about 20 US$) for the E-group or 50 guilders (about 30 US$) for the experimental groups. Subjects knew beforehand they had a 67% chance to be placed in the group with extra training and higher fee. Only after the experiment were they told to which group they belonged. All students had reached high math-levels at secondary school and had attended several mathematics or statistics courses after secondary school. Nearly all students had some experience in computer programming with half of the students more than 3 months full-time.

Materials

Materials for this experiment were the same as in the experiment of chapter 5 except for the following changes. The number of sentences in the instructional treatment has been reduced to 17 (see Appendix, Table A.8) and small changes in the general training have been made in order to shorten the introduction period. During the treatment students were now able to browse through the tasks. The explanatory text about the material conditional is partly a compilation and translation of the text that Cheng et al. (1986) have used in the rule training condition of their experiment 1, and partly a compilation and transla-

Table 6.1
Percentages correct on individual Wason selectiontasks for each condition

Testitem	Condition		
	TWG+E	TW+E	E
Cards			
pretest	28	17	22
posttest	44	39	67
follow-up	72	72	72
Blocks			
pretest	28	17	33
posttest	50	33	50
follow-up	56	72	56
Jars			
pretest	39	17	28
posttest	50	44	61
follow-up	72	83	83
Birds			
pretest	33	39	44
posttest	56	61	67
follow-up	50	56	61

Note. TW = Tarski's World, G = Game, E = Explanatory text. The first two items (Cards and Blocks) were counterbalanced. The third item was Jars and the fourth was Birds.

tion of the text about the conditional in the book that uses Tarski's World (Barwise & Etchemendy, 1990). See appendix Figures 10-13 for the full text.

Procedure
Subjects were randomly assigned to one of three conditions: (a) Tarski's World with the Game facility and formal explanation (TWG+E); (b) Tarski's World with formal explanation, but without the Game facility (TW+E); and (c) formal explanation condition only (E).

Subjects in groups of about 15 had to make a pretest with the four Wason selection tasks (about 6 minutes), and they had to do the Raven intelligence test (about 50 minutes). Then all received the first part of the general training for about two hours. Subjects were given the skill tests before the general training was fully accomplished.

Two to three weeks later subjects took up the second session individually. After some warming-up tasks they finished the general training in about half an hour and they received personal assistance when the results of the skill test were inadequate. Then all subjects received the text about the material conditional (about 7 minutes) after which the two experimental groups were given the

Table 6.2
PAC (Percentage All items Correct) on the far-transfer test for each condition

	Condition		
	TWG+E	TW+E	E
pretest	28	11	17
posttest	44	28	44
follow-up	50	50	33

Note. TW= Tarski's World, TWG=Tarski's World with Game, E= formal explanation. n = 18 for each condition.

instructional treatment (about 45 minutes). Afterwards all subjects had to make the near-transfer test and a far-transfer posttest (about 20 minutes).

In the third session, two to three weeks after the second session, all subjects, in groups of about 15, were exposed to a follow-up of the four Wason selection tasks (about 5 minutes).

Results

On the pretest the mean percentage correct for individual selection tasks is 29 (range 17 - 44 percent) over all conditions. The mean percentage on the posttest is 52 (range 33 - 67 percent) and on the follow-up it is 67 (range 43 - 83 percent). Mean percentages correct for each group and each item are presented in Table 6.1. Because four instead of two selection tasks were administered, the group percentages correct on all four Wason selection tasks (PAC) and the number of correct items (NC) could be used as dependent variables in addition to the logic indices (see section 4.4 for a description of PAC, NC and the logic index).

The effect of Game (comparing TWG+E with TW+E)

Immediate far-transfer effects (posttest - pretest). The two TW-conditions significantly increase 17% at the posttest on PAC (see Table 6.2), McNemar binomial test, $p < .05$, one-tailed. Although the TWG+E-group is advantaged on the pretest (PAC: 28 versus 11), and keeps that advantage on the posttest, the between-group differences are not significant, Pearson $\chi^2(1) < 1.60$. On NC (see Table 6.3), the increase is even clearer, $F(1,34) = 13.84$, $p < .001$, but again, there is no difference between conditions, $F(1,34) = .15$. On the most informative measure, the logic index (see Table 6.3), the increase is low (.25 for TWG+E and

Table 6.3
NC (number of correct items) and Logic indices on the far-transfer test for each condition

Dependent variables	Condition		
	TWG+E	TW+E	E
NC	M (SD)	M (SD)	M (SD)
pretest	1.28 (1.81)	.89 (1.41)	1.28 (1.60)
posttest	2.00 (1.97)	1.78 (1.73)	2.44 (1.72)
follow-up	2.50 (1.69)	2.83 (1.54)	2.72 (1.32)
Logic Index			
pretest	1.03 (.71)	1.03 (.49)	1.08 (.59)
posttest	1.28 (1.08)	1.08 (1.08)	1.56 (.49)
follow-up	1.38 (.71)	1.46 (.98)	1.43 (.81)

Note. TW= Tarski's World, TWG=Tarski's World with Game, E= formal explanation. n = 18 for each condition.

.06 for TW+E) and insignificant, $F(1,34) = 1.09$. Although the Game-condition improves more, the difference is insignificant, $F(1,34) = .44$.

Delayed far-transfer effects (follow up - pretest). On PAC, the delayed gain is 31%, McNemar test, $p < .001$, one-tailed. Both conditions have group scores of 50% on the follow-up. On NC, the difference in increase between groups (a small trend in favor of TW+E) is insignificant, $F(1,34) = 1.77$, $p = .19$, but the increase for both groups is large (from 1.1 to 2.7 items correct), $F(1,34) = 34.07$, $p < .001$. Logic indices show the same patterns (statistics are similar).

Near-transfer effects. The scores of the two TW groups on the near-transfer items (see Table 6.4) do not differ largely, apart from the SiD-item, on which the TWG+E-group scores 17% higher than the TW+E-group, although insignificant, Pearson $\chi^2(1) = 1.18$. The number of conditional errors on the near-transfer test is rather high and similar for both conditions (1.9 for TWG+E and 2.0 for TW+E), $F(1,33) = .14$.

The effect of Tarski's World instruction (comparing TW+E with E)

Immediate far-transfer effects (posttest - pretest). Both conditions improve on the posttest on PAC, McNemar binomial test, $p < .05$, one-tailed. The E-group scores 16 percent higher than TW-E on the posttest (see Table 6.2) and the E-group improves 10 percent more which is contrary to expectation (the trends are not significant, neither on the posttest, Pearson $\chi^2(1) = 1.08$, nor on the difference scores, Kruskal-Wallis $\chi^2(1) = .63$). On NC (see Table 6.3), subjects in both conditions improve from 1.1 items correct to 2.1 items, $F(1,34) = 17.89$, $p < .001$, while the difference (in favor of the E-group) between

Table 6.4
Percentages correct and the number of conditional errors
on the near-transfer test for each condition

	Condition		
	TWG+E	TW+E	E
Dependent variables	n = 18	n = 18	n = 19
% correct			
SiD&F-item	61	56	16
SiD-item	39	22	42
F-item	28	33	63
Conditional errors:			
M (SD)	1.88 (.99)	1.90 (.84)	1.89 (.94)

Note. TW = Tarski's World, SiD = situativity-in-domain, E = Explanatory text, F = Formal, G = Game.

conditions is insignificant, $F(1,34) = .33$. On the logic index (see Table 6.3), the increase ($F(1,34) = 3.82, p = .06$) is large (.47 points) for E and marginal (.06 points) for TW+E, but this difference is not significant, $F(1,34) = 2.38, p = .13$.

Delayed far-transfer effects (follow up - pretest). On PAC, the delayed gain is 39 percent (50 - 11), McNemar test, $p < .01$, one-tailed for TW+E and 16 percent (33 - 17) for the E condition, which is insignificant on the McNemar test. Differences between groups are insignificant both on the follow-up (50 versus 33 percent), Pearson $\chi^2(1) = 1.03, p = .16$, and the difference scores (39 versus 16 percent), Kruskal-Wallis $\chi^2(1) = 1.15, p = .14$. Improvement on NC is 1.7 (2.8 - 1.1) items for both groups, $F(1,34) = 41.16, p < .001$. Between-groups difference (in favor of TW+E) is insignificant, $F(1,34) = .90$. Gain in logic indices are substantial for both conditions ($F(1,34) = 7.68, p < .01$) but only marginally (.43 versus .35 points, $F(1,34) = .09$) higher for the TW+E-condition.

Near-transfer effects. Although the frequencies of conditional errors (see Table 6.4) on the near-transfer test do no differ between conditions (2.0 for TW+E and 1.9 for E), $F(1,35) = .13$, large differences are found on percentages correct for individual items. There is a large effect on the SiD&F-item (53 versus 16 percent in favor of TW+E), Pearson $\chi^2(1) = 6.41, p < .01$, but for the other items the trend is the counterexpected (the E-group gives 20 and 30 percent more correct answers on resp. SiD and F items), although insignificant ($\chi^2(1) = 3.29, p = .07$ for the F-item, $\chi^2(1) = 1.67$ for the SiD-item).

Discussion

These results are striking as subjects already improve on the selection tasks only after exposure to a short formal text. Based on the abundant literature on the abstract or arbitrary selection task (see chapter 3), this effect was totally unexpected. Only on the theoretically strongest variable (PAC on the follow-up), the experimental groups proved to have gained a stable and logically correct response to the selection tasks while the control group, with only explanatory text, failed to do so. Both results, the baseline trend of the control condition and the delayed experimental trend are important and require further discussion concerning the potential factors involved.

Based on post-hoc analyses and considerations, it will be argued below that the instructional treatment may inhibit learning initially, and that the instructional effect may be subject to a sort of incubation period. The improvement of the control group indicates that the effect of prior formal experience is stronger than expected for this (sub)population.

A Possible Effect of Inhibition

The TW groups improve (posttest) on PAC and NC but on the Logic index the improvement is only moderately. This signals that students who do not produce correct answers, actually impede after treatment. For the subset of subjects (n = 31) who do not improve on NC (posttest), the TWG+E- and the E-groups neither gain nor lose on the logic index, resp. -.02 ($SD = .77$) and .03 ($SD = .34$) points difference, in contrast to the TW+E group which impedes strongly with .42 ($SD = 1.13$). However, the difference between groups is not significant, $F(2,28) = .86$.

Although the supposed inhibition has no statistical back-up, analyses of the number of correct translated sentences during the treatment makes clear that a substantial number of subjects did have problems with the treatment. Although 45 percent of the subjects were able to produce correct translations (at most one error in 17 sentences), a substantial 19 percent of the subjects did not address more than 11 sentences, meaning that they skipped the last two or three problems. Only 75 percent of the subjects (no significant between-group difference) completed the instructional treatment, that is, all sentences have been translated and verified, regardless of the correctness of the translation. This is remarkable as in the experiment of chapter 5 as much as 98 percent of the TW-group of chapter 5 completed the instructional treatment. Subjects who became pressed for time generally had been working for a long time on the third problem. This problem is crucial as it introduces quantified conditional expressions. A plausible explanation for the difference between the social science students of the experiment of chapter 5 and the technical science students in this experiment is the experience with formal systems. The more experienced, technical science students may have been trying to apply their prior knowledge during the instructional treatment, especially when the truth value of a sentence is counterintuitive. The less experienced social science students were more likely to continue the treatment after such experiences

Another sign for inhibition is whether subjects consulted other persons after treatment (they were explicitly asked not to do so) concerning the treatment or the Wason selection task. It may be expected that subjects who are highly disturbed[3] by the experiences are more likely to consult other subjects than those who are not disturbed. On a questionaire taken after the follow-up, 24 percent of the TW+E-group responded that they did consult others against 6 percent for the TWG+E- and E-groups. When these students were excluded from the analyses the inhibition trend on the posttest disappears while the trends on the follow-up remained the same.

A Possible Effect of Explanation

The result that merely formal explanation facilitates logical reasoning on the selection tasks is contrary to the findings of Cheng et al. (1986). However, a closer look on individual testitems shows that formal explanation may not have been the only facilitative factor. The first selection task (not necessarily Cards) was solved by 24 percent of the sample, which is rather high from the start. Group percentages already improve substantially during the third and fourth items of the pretest, meaning that with each item, more students may have seen the fit between the rule in the task and the material conditional. During the first eight selection tasks (pretest and posttest) there is a strong relationship between the number of tasks and the performance ($r = .96$, $p < .001$, for the E-group). The treatment does not seem to influence the regression line strongly, although there may be a small effect of the treatment (see Figure 6.1): Taken together, the first eight items show a general increase of 6.5 percent for each subsequent item while the increase during the pretest is 4.9 percent per item and the increase

---

[3]The experiences are disturbing because they do not accord with the 'logic' of everyday life: Most people will use some kind of Pragmatic Reasoning Schema (or a specific neural reasoning network), which has been induced through earlier everyday-life experiences, to solve the tasks. Formal logic sometimes conflicts with such less abstract reasoning schema's. The instructional treatment has been developed specifically to acquaint students with situations in which the two logics conflict. As the feedback provided by Tarski's World accords with formal logic, the assumed neural reasoning networks are literally disturbed. However, the Game can be seen as a conflict-resolver as the student learns or is reminded of the fact that a conditional expression is equivalent to a certain disjunction in formal logic.

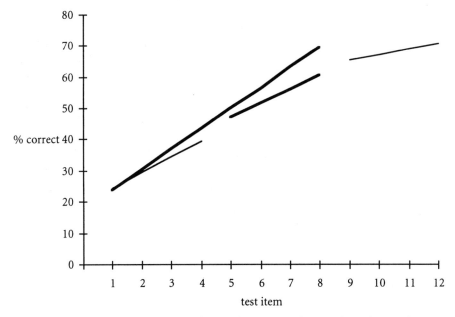

Figure 6.1. Regression lines for the far-tranfer testitems (E-group). Fat lines indicate significance ($p < .01$) of both slope and height.

during the posttest is 4.4 percent per item. During the follow-up, group performance on individual tasks barely improves: It fluctuates around 67 percent, indicating that the group has reached its ceiling.

The percentages correct on individual selection tasks as well as NC and the logic index seem to reflect the prior tendency of the subjects to reason logically more than that they reflect an effect of instruction, at least for this (sub)population. PAC, although not independent of the other measures, is more sensitive to the treatment effects as it reflects the proportion of subjects with a stable and correct understanding during a test. PAC shows a trend that the effect of a formal text does not last and that the interaction of the formal text with TW-instruction has a delayed effect.

Conclusions about the effect of the formal explanation cannot be drawn. The difference in gain of the E-group and the TW+E-group may be attributed to facilitation of the formal instruction, to inhibition of TW+E-instruction, or to an interaction of both effects.

An Effect of Incubation

A possible cause for the delayed facilitation, as measured with PAC, may be derived from the developmental situativity theory: The neural networks who work on conditional reasoning may be highly activated during the treatment, but as these networks try to process confronting information they may not be able to settle down yet (knowledge within connectionism is represented non-symbolically by settled patterns of distibuted activation in networks). Even when not consciously thinking about it, the disturbed reasoning networks may work towards a new equilibrium and are therefore sensitive to several kinds of information and may settle down only when critical information arrives. This too is considered to be part of induction. When exposed again to the selection tasks after days or weeks, the activated networks may settle down quickly and consistently to logic.[4]

Near-transfer effects

The nearly equal score of the E group on the SiD-item and the higher one on the F-item is a surprising result. A lower score was expected on the SiD&F- and the F-items as the E-group has not been trained in formulating *conditional* expressions in logic. A lower score on the SiD-item was expected because of the only-explanatory training that the E-group received. In general, the near-transfer test was made badly: nearly two conditional errors in three items is not a good score for the TW-groups. It signals again that TW-instruction may have been inhibiting outcomes.

Concluding Remarks

Again, as in chapter 5, firm conclusions on the effectivity of the instructional treatment cannot be reached. Yet, important results were found. The intermediate experienced students in formal systems already improve on subsequent selection tasks even before instruction starts. Such an effect was unexpected as abundant research on arbitrary selection tasks proved that subjects do not improve, neither on subsequent tasks nor after instruction (see chapter 3). Only Cheng et al (1986) and Lehman et al. (1990) found instructional effects on arbitrary tasks, but the effect in the Cheng et al experiment is a near-transfer effect and the effect of the Lehman et al. study was found after a long period of formal instruction. The effect was unexpected too as the pilot study (chapter 5),

---

[4]Such speculations naturally should be 'proved' somehow. Empirical data, as presented here is considered to be too weak for this. It is a combination of simulations of such processes and empirical data that may supply the theory with enough credibility.

with a comparable sample of technical science students, did not reveal the effect, possibly because the test (with only two items) was insensitive to it. Most subjects may have had some initial understanding of the material conditional but many of those were not able to apply it to the selection tasks directly. Repeated exposure to the task was sufficient to improve substantively for the intermediate experienced students. Therefore, in further research, it is important to use students who are less experienced with formal systems (as provided in courses for mathematics, computer science, statistics).

Instruction with explanatory text facilitates reasoning at most marginally while the interaction of explanatory text with Tarski's World may be inhibitory directly after instruction. It is difficult to determine whether a temporary inhibition signals a positive or a negative effect of instruction. It may be argued that instruction which is based on confrontation with the counterintuitive, keeps disturbing students for some period after the instruction in associated tasks. Such an effect may be part of the incubation hypothesis. Some educational scholars, perhaps, would state that proper instruction should not let students go away disturbed, whatever confronting experiences the students may have had. The question whether inhibition is positive or negative in theory or ethics does not have to be answered until it is ruled out that the possible inhibition does not stem from instructional faults. For the next experiment, the third task in the instructional treatment should be re-analyzed as it appears to be a bottleneck for one in every five students.

The Wason selection task seems to be a very critical task for which the period in which a measurable learning-effect can be established may be rather short (depending on prior formal experience). The sub-population of second- and third-year technical science students proves to be almost beyond this period, as only the theoretically strongest, but statistically weakest measure, PAC, reveals a positive delayed effect of Tarski's World instruction. Although the present experiment does not provide a final answer to the question whether a combination of formal text and Tarski's World-instruction is effective, the effect on PAC and the spontaneous improvement of intermediate experienced students is important and feeds optimism for further research with the same test, with less experienced subjects, and perhaps with a slightly revised instructional treatment.

7

Situativity versus Formality in Logic Instruction Part 2

7.1 Introduction

The experiments of chapters 5 and 6 have not produced answers to their research questions as several unforeseen disturbing factors were too influential. In all experiments some problem of time-pressure has been noticed, although it was only clearly defective in the pilot study. In chapter 5, it was found that the instructional treatment was insufficiently strong to improve results on the Wason selection tasks, at least for the particular subpopulation: students with minor experience in mathematics. An explanatory text concerning the material conditional was added to the instructional treatment in the following experiment (chapter 6) which was designed to measure the effect of Tarski's World instruction above the otherwise ineffective text. It proved that intermediate experienced subjects used in the sample could improve even without the instructional treatment. The influence of prior knowledge or experience in previous experiments is related to an aspect of Vygotsky's developmental psychology to which no explicit attention has been paid so far: the zone of proximal development (Vygotsky, 1934/1987, pp. 209-214).

When a person is unable to solve a problem independently, but a solution can be found with some help, the person is in its Zone of Proximal Development (ZPD) for that type of problem. For Vygotsky, the ZPD is a most important concept for (the design of) instruction (Vygotsky, p. 210):

> A central feature for the psychological study of instruction is the analysis of the child's potential to raise himself to a higher intellectual level of development through collaboration, to move from what he has to what he does not have through imitation. This is the significance of instruction for development. It is also the content of the concept of the zone of proximal development.

Instruction should not simply be led by the state of prior knowledge of students, by their actual development, but instead by their potential to go beyond that stage. Two eight-year-old children with an actual development of that age (i.e., normal and identical IQ's) may differ largely in their ZPD: In collaboration, one child may be able to solve problems which normally can only be solved by twelve-year-olds, while the other may not be able to go beyond problems which can be solved by nine-year-olds. Within the ZPD, formal concepts (used in reflective activity) can be related appropriately to everyday concepts (used in experiential, situated activity) when some *help system* is provided (see Vygotsky, p. 220).

Vygotsky's conception of a help system may be too limited for powerful instruction. *Natural* help —as proposed by Vygotsky— like demonstration or collaboration, most likely leads to near-transfer effects only. *Artificial* systems, e.g., interactive computer programs like Tarski's World, provide for a help system in a more abstract sense: A formal system with an accompanying situated-learning environment. Using an artificial help system may establish an appropriate relation between the two systems of concepts —formal and everyday— involved. The use of artificial help systems provides for those experiences and tools that are supposed to be necessary for far-transfer effects.

Till so far, it has been assumed implicitly that any undergraduate (or any intelligent adult) is in the ZPD for reasoning in the Wason selection task,[1] which means that, in principle, all students were assumed to be able to reason conform to formal logic after appropriate instruction. The results of the previous experiments strongly suggest that this assumption is false. The social science students probably were not yet in the ZPD for the selection task. Without subjects in the ZPD, Tarski's World cannot be effective. In contrast, the intermediate experienced technical science students were able to improve even without the instructional treatment, and consequently treatment effects were weak. Many of these students appeared to be just beyond the ZPD for reasoning in the Wason selection task. In the present experiment a subpopulation will be used that is more experienced than first-year social science students and less experienced than second- or third-year technical science students: first-year

---

[1]When ZPD is defined in the broader sense, artificial instructional systems are accepted as help providers too. Help fails when using natural help as demonstration (see chapter 3).

technical science students in the second half of their college year. It is expected that many of these students will be in the ZPD for the selection task.

The ZPD for a specific domain clearly depends on prior knowledge, but not on this alone. Intelligence, motivation and the ability to make new tools profitable (which is different from intelligence as Vygotsky demonstrated) are also candidates for ZPD-determinants. However, only prior knowledge will be used as an operationalization for the ZPD, as this is sufficient for the present experimental design in which only between-group differences count.

Prior knowledge of formal systems is supposed to be a major factor within previous experiments, but some instructional effects, although suppressed by this factor and therefore statistically weak, may already have introduced themselves: The explanatory text seems to have a temporary positive effect only, while the instructional treatment (in addition to the text) seems to have an immediate inhibitory effect (given the effect of the only-explanation treatment as a base-line) and a positive delayed effect. A plausible cause for the inhibitory effect may be a difficulty within the instructional treatment which is not an important instructional element (see Method section below). The instructional treatment has been altered in order to remove this problem. The explanatory formal text does not stimulate inductive processes by itself, but it may function as a catalyst when other instruction allows for such inductive processes. It is assumed that students who have not passed the ZPD yet, cannot learn from formal texts without situated action. Tarski's World stimulates such activity. While working, students may compare the formalized knowledge with their experiences. Although the effect of the Game may be suppressed too by the prior knowledge factor in chapter 6, the Game does not appear to be very influential and, therefore, there is no need to use the Game facility in the present experiment.

The central question in this study can now be addressed again: Is the combination of Situativity-in-Domain (SiD) and formal aspects within each learning moment a prerequisite for effective and efficient instruction or can only-SiD or only-formal instruction be productive too? Compared to the experiments in chapter 5, there are some changes —apart from several small improvements— , noticably the addition of the explanatory text. Besides its function as a catalyst, the text functions as overview of the domain through which the attention of subjects is clearly driven to the material conditional. Both functions are top-down elements in a further bottom-up, inductive learning process.

7.2. Method

Subjects

80 Technical first-year students of the University of Twente (63 male, 17 female; mean age 19.4 years, $SD = 1.6$) volunteered for the experiment. Most students had reached a high math-level at secondary school, after which they have had some experience or training in mathematics and computer programming. The experiment was presented as a free one-day introduction in formal logic with a paid experimental part. Subjects in the experimental groups were paid 50 Dutch guilders (about 30 US$); subjects in the control group were paid 35 Dutch guilders (about 20 US$). Subjects, who were allocated randomly to conditions, knew beforehand they had a 75% chance to be placed in a group with longer instruction and higher fee. They were told only after the experiment to which group they belonged.

Materials

All subjects in the experimental groups received a text about the material conditional and 6 Tarski's World problems containing altogether 18 sentences in natural language (see Appendix, Table A.1). Subjects in the control group received neither the text nor the problems. The tests are identical to the tests used in chapter 6 (for a description see section 4.4, and Appendix, Table A.3 and Figures A.6 - A.9)).

Compared to the version used in chapter 6, the explanatory text has been made less formal. A very formal text would possibly distort the only-SiD nature of the TW^{SiD}-condition, making it a partial SiD&F-condition. Although it is assumed that the strongest result will be gained by experiences in which SiD is combined with formality, a few students may be able to successfully connect the SiD-experience with the formal text that has been read earlier even without formality during the experience. An explanatory text is now considered to be a necessary catalyst, but it is kept as concretely as possible to keep the TW^{SiD}-condition as less formal as possible (see Appendix, Figures A.1-4).

The instructional treatment has been altered in order to diminish the possible inhibitory effect as signaled in chapter 6. This alleged inhibition may have been caused by the disturbing but desired experiences with Tarski's World instruction, but it may also have been caused by the unusual logical expression used in the testitems SiD&F and SiD and preparatory to the test in task D of the instructional treatment (see Appendix, Tables A.2 and A.6). It concerns sentences of the form "There is something for which it holds that if it is an A, statement B is true". These sentences can easily be mistaken for sentences of the form "If there is an A, statement B is true". As instruction was designed fully to facilitate experiences by the subject, no further comments or explanation were made to guide subjects to the difference between these sentences, although they have to understand the difference between the two forms in order to complete task 3 successfully. It was found that a substantial proportion of the subjects were having problems with this task (chapter 6). In the present instruction, the differences will be pointed out more explicitely to the subjects.

Procedure

Subjects were randomly assigned to one of four conditions: (1) TW-instruction (SiD&F-group) (2) TW^{SiD}-instruction (SiD-group), (3) TW^F-instruction (F-group), and (4) a control condition in which no instruction beyond the general training is presented (C-group). The experiment was held in two sessions, one session of 3 to 5 hours and a second session of 5 minutes. Sessions took place in groups of at most five subjects (all subjects worked individually). In the first session subjects had to make a pretest with the four Wason selection tasks (about 5 minutes). Then all subjects received the general training for about 2 hours. After a lunchbreak, subjects continued the general training for about 1 hour after which they had to make the skill test. When a subject did not complete the test items within 10 minutes, he or she received personal assistance. After the skill-test subjects in the control group had to make a posttest with the Wason selection tasks, other subjects received the instructional treatment (about 60 minutes). After instruction in conditional reasoning the subjects had to do the near-transfer test and a posttest of the far-transfer test (about 20 minutes). A week later, the second session took place which only contained a follow-up of the far-transfer test.

7.3 Results

Immediate far-transfer effects (posttest - pretest)

The overall increase on PAC is 16% (19% - 3%, see Table 7.1), which is significant, McNemar binomial test $p < .001$. However, for individual groups, differences were found significant only for the SiD&F-group (30% improvement), McNemar test, $p < .05$, one-tailed. Differences in PAC increase between all groups is not significant, Kruskal-Wallis $\chi^2 = 4.63$, $p = .20$. Comparing individual groups revealed only a significant difference between the SiD&F-

Table 7.1
PAC (Percentage All items Correct) on the far-transfer test for each condition

Dependent variables	Condition			
	TW	TWSiD	TWF	C
pretest	0	0	5	5
posttest	30	15	20	10
follow-up	50	20	20	15

Note. TW = Tarski's World, SiD = Situativity-in-Domain, F = formal, C = Control. n = 20 for each group.

group and the C-group in favor of the SiD&F-group (25% difference in gain), χ^2 = 4.22, $p < .05$.

Logic indices and NC (see Table 7.2) show the same patterns as PAC (using repeated measures with contrasts for comparing individual groups).[2] The overall increase of the logic index is .31 points, $F(1,76) = 19.48$, $p < .001$. No significant gain-difference is found between all groups, $F(3,76) = 1.11$, $p = .35$. Comparing individual groups, only the .36 points gain-difference between the SiD&F-group and the C-group is found to be significant, $F(1,76) = 3.28$, $p < .05$.

Delayed far-transfer effects (follow-up - pretest)

The overall gain in PAC of 25% (see Table 7.1) is significant, McNemar test, $p < .001$. Improvement for individual groups is significant for the SiD&F-group (50%), McNemar test, $p < .001$, one-tailed. The 20% improvement for the SiD-group is not significant, McNemar test, $p = .06$, one-tailed. PAC increase differs between groups, $\chi^2 = 9.40$, $p < .05$. This difference can be attributed to differences between the SiD&F-group and the other groups, for SiD&F versus SiD and SiD&F versus F (resp. 30% and 35% more increase for the SiD&F-group) $\chi^2 > 3.85$, $p < .05$, for SiD&F versus C (40% more increase for the SiD&F-group) $\chi^2 = 7.43$, $p < .01$. Differences in PAC increase between SiD, F, and C groups are not significant, $\chi^2 < .77$.

The overall increase of the logic index (see Table 7.2) is .46 points, which is significant, $F(1,76) = 51.75$, $p < .001$. Gain-difference between the groups is not significant, $F(3,76) = 2.57$, $p = .06$. However, comparing individual groups, it is found that SiD&F versus SiD and SiD&F versus F differences in gain (resp. .38 and .39 points more increase for the SiD&F-group) are significant on the 5% level, $F(1,76) > 4.31$, and that SiD&F versus C difference (.46 points more

---

[2] As conlusions are the same for NC and the Logic index, only the analyses with the logic index are reported).

Table 7.2
NC (Number of Correct items) and logic indices
on the far-transfer test for each condition

Dependent variables	Condition			
	TW	TWSiD	TWF	C
NC	M (SD)	M (SD)	M (SD)	M (SD)
pretest	.55 (.89)	.20 (.47)	.70 (1.13)	.55 (.88)
posttest	1.60 (1.76)	1.00 (1.52)	1.00 (1.62)	.80 (1.44)
follow-up	2.20 (1.94)	1.20 (1.61)	1.20 (1.67)	1.30 (1.53)
Logic index				
pretest	.71 (.70)	.74 (.30)	.76 (.67)	.70 (.55)
posttest	1.21 (.65)	1.06 (.51)	1.05 (.59)	.84 (.63)
follow-up	1.48 (.60)	1.13 (.59)	1.14 (.59)	1.01 (.63)

Note. TW = Tarski's World, SiD = Situativity-in-Domain, F = formal, C = Control. n = 20 for each group.

increase for the SiD&F-group) is significant on the 1% level, $F(1,76) = 6.21$. Differences in increase on the logic index between SiD, F and C groups are not significant, $F(1,76) < .18$.

Near-transfer test

Group differences in percentages correct are in line with hypotheses for the SiD&F- and SiD-items and for the number of conditional errors (see Table 7.3). SiD&F-group scored highest on both tasks and the SiD-group scores higher than the F-group on the SiD-item. The SiD&F-group makes fewest conditional errors on the test directly followed by the SiD-group. The F-group made most errors. However, none of these group differences are significant ($F(2,57) = 1.16$, $p = .21$ for the frequency of conditional errors, Pearson $\chi^2(2) = 4.23$, $p = .12$ for the item with the largest differences, the SiD-item). Also, most differences between groups do not reach significance either ($t(38) = 1.63$, $p = .06$, for the SiD&F- versus F-groups on the number of conditional errors, $\chi^2(1) = 2.67$, $p = .05$, for SiD&F versus SiD and SiD&F versus F on the SiD&F-item). Only the 25% difference between the SiD&F- and F-groups on the SiD-item is significant, $\chi^2(1) = 4.3$, $p < .05$. Tendencies on the F-item are contrary to expectations: the SiD-group scores better than the other groups, but insignificantly.

Table 7.3
Percentages correct and the number of conditional errors on the near-transfer test for each condition

Dependent variables	Condition		
	TW	TW^{SiD}	TW^F
% correct			
SiD&F-item	50	25	25
SiD-item	30	20	5
F-item	40	60	40
Conditional errors:			
M (SD)	1.75 (.97)	1.85 (.75)	2.20 (.77)

Note. TW = Tarski's World, SiD = Situativity-in-Domain, F = formal.

7.4 Discussion

The results show, as hypothesized, a facilitating effect of TW-instruction on the Wason selection tasks, directly after the treatment and even stronger after a week (50% all items correct against 15% for the control group).[3] Conform the hypotheses, only-SiD instruction and only-formal instruction do not enhance logical reasoning more than the control group does. These findings illustrate the importance of a combined SiD and formal instruction. An only-SiD instruction is not effective, because it lacks the tools to abstract from the experiences beyond the near-transfer level. This demonstrates the incompleteness of the induction framework of Holland et al. (1986). An only-formal instruction is not effective as it only provides tools without the situations in which the tools can be used relevantly.

The improvement of the control group on the Wason selection tasks (especially on the logic index and NC) indicates that few students were already beyond the ZPD. Without *any* instruction on conditional reasoning, these

---

[3]Post-hoc analysis of the selection tasks data signals a possible effect of gender. Female students tend to score lower than male students on the pretest. On the posttest and the follow-up, women in the SiD&F and SiD groups score higher than men. Also, the gain for women is higher than for men in all groups. Although the difference in gain between male and female students tends to be largest in the SiD&F-group (.46 points on the logic index) and negligible in the control group (.04 points), no significant interaction of condition, sex, and testphase has been found. The directions of the female-trends are not different from the male-trends, where the effects are strong too. For the SiD&F and SiD groups, the effects seem to be stronger for female students. For further study it is thought to be wise to control for this possible gender-effect.

students give correct answers or withdraw errors after repeated presentation of the Wason selection task, although often not consistently yet. These students are believed to be ready to see the significance of the modus tollens due to their formal studies. Some additional support to the explanation of the ZPD is that nearly half of the students who think they understand the material conditional attribute this partly or totally to mathematics courses they have followed, according to a questionnaire given after the posttest.

Results are not conclusive for the near-transfer test. The SiD&F-group and the only-SiD group tend to perform better than the only-formal group, but a larger sample or a more discriminative test is needed to confirm this expected trend statistically.

PART IV
Discussion

8

General Discussion and Epilogue

8.1 Conclusion and Value of this Study

In this thesis the unique general psychology of Vygotsky has been combined with a new paradigm in cognitive science, situated action. The resulting developmental situativity theory assumes an intimate relation between situative and formal aspects of learning. This theory is considered to be important for instructional science because it proclaims that instruction is only powerful (i.e., efficient and effective) when both aspects of learning, situativity-in-domain (SiD) and formality, are connected in a single instructional experience (in which the processing of feedback is the central element). This notion gave the impetus to a series of experiments with Tarski's World, which was recognized as facilitating SiD while providing formal tools to introduce students to formal logic. The instructional treatment in this study was designed for a specific purpose: The facilitation of logical conditional reasoning. Support was found for the hypothesis that a combination of SiD and formal instruction is more productive than either SiD or formal instruction alone, but it was subject to more constraints than expected. An explanatory text concerning the material conditional seemed to be necessary and the effect only appeared when using students with moderate experience in mathematics as subjects.

The theory as presented in chapter 2 may appear to be somewhat speculative in the eyes of cognitivist readers. However, as the basic assumptions of situated action operate on a paradigmatic level, the speculation is not different in nature from, e.g., the cognitivistic assumption that human beings process symbols with a central processing unit. The matter boils down to a question of worldview to which one may or may not adapt (Agre, 1993). As a worldview alone is too broad for direct theoretical and empirical progression, more specific theories have to be proposed. Early situated action theories (e.g., Suchman, 1987; Brown, Collins & Duguid, 1989) lacked a psychological point of view. Therefore, in chapter 2, it has been tried to provide for a psychological version of situated action which is based on the developmental psychology of Vygotsky. To combine situated action theory with the developmental psychology of Vygotsky consistently, an additional constructivistic element was introduced to Vygotsky's theory saying that any concept, either everyday or formal, cannot be construed objectively. Vygotsky, in my reading, saw the development of formal concepts as an enterprise of society in reaching objectivity. The weakness of the resulting theory is not that it is speculative, but that it is not yet very specific.

Specific theories may be derived from a theory as global as the developmental situativity theory of chapter 2, but considerable effort will be needed before they will be backboned by empirical data. Especially the early studies within a new paradigm may be based on trial and error before the demands of the theories can be understood and new methods and techniques can be constructed to meet those demands. I have tried to avoid such trial and error research by searching a topic that would demonstrate a central issue of the developmental situativity theory very directly in a simple experimental design by means of Tarski's World and its impaired versions. The topic of learning conditional reasoning was suitable for this purpose because Tarski's World clearly 'affords' the activity of subjects that is necessary to experience the meaning of the logical conditional. Furthermore, the literature on abstract conditional reasoning is negative concerning a learning effect, but the type of instruction that is possible with Tarski's World has never been used. After succeeding, more specific learning and reasoning theories could be developed. This research plan was too optimistic as the chapters 5, 6 and 7 reveal. Only after considerable ad hoc theorizing and trial and error concerning several methodological, technical, and instructional issues —a systematic approach would have been excessively expensive— , the constraints within which a learning effect could be measured were found. Only after three preliminary studies, support for the initial hypothesis was gained.

Despite the pilot status of most material in this thesis and the constraints under which the main hypothesis was finally supported, the successful manipulation of a crucial learning moment in the fundamental but refractory subject of conditional reasoning is of general importance. It is concluded that the *dual stimulation*[1] of situative and formal elements within each instructional event[2] is a conditio sine qua non for effective and efficient instruction in conditional reasoning, provided that the learner is in the zone of proximal development. In the next sections, I will reflect more specifically on several implications of the developmental situativity theory and the results of the present study, and I will prelude on the research needed for further progression.

8.2 Theoretical Implications

For the psychology of reasoning, the developmental situativity theory does not provide a specific theory. However, to my opinion, such a theory would not be very deviant to the Pragmatic Reasoning Schema theory (Cheng & Holyoak, 1985), in contrast to the theories which lean strongly on logic, using either syntactics (natural logics) or semantics (mental models) as their bases. Other human reasoning theories have been rejecting the notion that there is a general reasoning mechanism and assume reasoning to be fully dependent on domain specific information. Early situated action theories, e.g., Suchman's anthropological study (1987), appear to be consistent to the domain specificity theory, but I consider this is a side-effect of her objective to demonstrate the primary role of situativity in everyday life. There are certainly domain-specific elements in reasoning, but people are also able to abstract from such domains, provided that such abstractions are useful (some formalities may be useful in some societies but not in others). The position that people induce abstractions based on their experiences and expected utilities, not on pure syntactic rules, is a pragmatic one. This position is taken in both the Pragmatic Reasoning Schema (PRS) theory as well as in the developmental situativity theory. The PRS theory is embedded in the Induction framework (Holland et al., 1986) and concerns special types of inference rules. The developmental situativity theory lies on the same level as the Induction framework and lacks the specificity of the PRS theory. Broadly, this thesis can be seen as a comparison between both theories or frameworks with respect to the induction of a deductive rule: The modus tollens as associated with the material conditional.

---

[1] I use this Vygotskian expression in a different, but analogous context. Vygotsky uses the term to refer to a research method for studying developmental processes in children: one series of stimuli concerns simple or complex tasks, a second series of stimuli (simultaneously provided or advised to be created by the child itself) concerns tools that can be used for solving the tasks.

[2] Any intended activity to promote learning that includes feedback to the students activity.

Within both theories, the material conditional is believed to have limited pragmatic value in everyday life (see Holland et al. pp. 234, 283).[3] However, the material conditional could become a PRS when people are placed into several situations in which real-life experiences are possible, but in which only the logical definition of the conditional is appropriate. This provides a competitive field for the formal conditional and the leading pragmatic conditionals. When the provided feedback is clearly and consistently against the leading pragmatic conditionals, the student will have to adapt to the material conditional in order to succeed. This scenario would facilitate logical reasoning according to both theories. The problem is that in real-life these situations hardly occur, at least not consistently enough. Therefore, they have to be simulated somehow. Tarski's World provides an appropriate competitive field by using an interactive graphical representation of situations in which only the logical interpretation is correct. Both theories are positive on the success of Tarski's World, perhaps not for all everyday life situations in which conditional expressions are used and perhaps not for a long time, but at least when confronted with the Wason selection task.

Although both theories are positive on the instructional potential of Tarski's World, the developmental situativity theory and the induction framework differ in their instructional prescriptions for what is needed to succeed. The induction framework does not make a fundamental distinction between everyday concepts and formal concepts.[4] Consequently, the symbol systems used in Tarski's World, the natural language (as used in the program) and the interpreted first-order logic, are believed to be equivalent, which makes one of them redundant. In contrast, the developmental situativity theory defines the natural language used in Tarski's World as a language functional for everyday concepts which makes it situated, while the logic language is too

---

[3]For example, the Raven paradox: The statement "All ravens are black" is logically equivalent to "All non-black things are non-ravens". Thus, the statement "All ravens are black" can be confirmed with a white shoe. This is nonsense in everyday life. Note that the Instructional Treatment can be seen as a repeated exposure to the Raven paradox. Another example: It may be true that "if the power hadn't failed, dinner would have been on time"; but it doesn't follow --in everyday life-- that "if dinner had not been on time, then the power would have failed". In logic, however, it does.

[4]The induction framework does make a difference between folk definitions and technical definitions of concepts and the latter may be used in instruction to ensure theory-guided induction (Holland et al. p. 191). However, the distinction concerns the quality of the definition, not its nature. In my view, folk definitions can be based on complexes (in Vygotsky's terms), or on abstractions which are often scientifically incorrect. Therefore, folk definitions can be situated or formal in nature. The technical definition is a result of scientific effort and consequently formal in nature. In the induction framework, folk definitions and technical definitions are both formal.

artificial for this purpose. In this thesis logic functions as a tool for discovering the logical meaning of the conditionals as expressed in both languages. Meaning in the concrete, natural language is situated and without the use of tools it cannot be changed (for people who have not passed the zone of proximal development). Therefore, the developmental situativity theory predicts the need for both languages, one for the interactive graphical experiences and one as a tool. The empirical results of this thesis provide support for the developmental situativity theory and demonstrate a fundamental limitation of the Induction framework.

Do the results discredit the induction framework? To some extent they do, but because many notions of the induction framework are in accord with the developmental situativity theory, I prefer to see the Induction framework as an abstracted, weak cognitivistic version of the developmental situativity theory. I suggest not to reject the induction framework, but instead to reframe it into a situated action theory. As the induction framework is pragmatic —it relieves induction from a formal logical approach— , it will only be consistent to be pragmatic concerning the structure of information upon which inductive processes operate. A reframing requires at least three main activities: First, the different functions of everyday concepts and formal concepts will have to be operationalized. Second, the induction framework assumes that the system is able to use formal concepts from the start. From the developmental situativity perspective, this is not a realistic assumption. Therefore, the qualitative changes of inductive processes during development will have to be taken into account. Third, computational aspects of situativity will have to be worked out.

It may be illustrative to give an idea of the computational demands of a developmental situativity theory in relation to contemporary computational paradigms. In a situativity theoretical prospect, classical artificial intelligence -based on production rules and an inference engine- is a dead end, due to its one-sided formality. So is pure connectionism for its one-sided situativity (it should be possible to simulate non-reflecting life forms though). Hybrid forms of symbolic and connectionistic models may be more powerful than either symbolic or connectionistic models, but the relation between the two parts is a static one and that forms a bottleneck for intelligence (only within a very narrow range of tasks may such systems produce adaptive and 'intelligent' behavior). In contrast, computational situativity models should be robotics which is based on a connectionistic-like architecture that restructures itself during Vygotskian stages of development. The problems in this enterprise are immense, but the search for artificial intelligence will no longer be purely technology driven. There will be several clear psychological constraints to work with and to head for. Naturally, it is neither possible nor wishful to rebuilt a human being electronically or optically. At any rate, the psychological reality of robots will be quite different from ours.

8.3 Research Implications

This study revealed an interesting and important learning effect in deductive reasoning. However, the developmental situativity theory guiding the research is a global theory which cannot be proved by means of a single experiment. Furthermore, the learning effect has been found only once after preliminary research was performed, which may not be sufficient to convince a skeptic community of reasoning researchers immediately. After all, research with arbitrary Wason selection tasks has been performed for nearly 30 years now, which has lead to a reserved attitude towards learning possibilities. Therefore, more work has to be done to provide the theory and the research with the necessary credibility. In this section, I will make some suggestions about how to achieve such credibility.

The obvious thing to do is to replicate the experiment of chapter 7. However, I suggest several changes in order to resolve some uncertainties and to sharpen the hypothesis. Conform the hypothesis that SiD and formal elements are both needed within each instructional event, it was found that neither an only-SiD instruction nor an only-formal instruction is effective. The same hypothesis can also be tested by using two series of instructional events in one condition, one series based on only-SiD instruction and another series based on only-formal instruction. There are several ways to design the instructional treatment for this condition, but an important constraint is that tasks within each series should be different in order to prevent that the subject is able to combine the feedback of both tasks into a conclusion for the second task. Despite several difficulties and limitations, a subject who tries to combine the two feedback moments creates one event out of two.

The functions of prior knowledge or experience and the ZPD are not very clear yet. Variables as secondary school mathematics level, experience in computer programming, and the number of attended formal courses are not very helpful for explaining logic index variances within a sample,[5] although Lehman and Nisbett (1990) refer to the amount of formal education to explain the facilitation of logical reasoning in the Wason selection task of some groups. However, differences between cohorts of students seem to be very important in

---

[5]These variables were measured primarily to control for pretest differences between conditions as randomizing procedures might not have been sufficient for the relatively small group sizes.. However, no significant difference was found in any experiment.

this thesis, but unfortunately, the different experiments are not fully comparable to each other due to differences in instruction and experimental design. Future research should control for variances concerning prior knowledge or experience more systematically. However, controlling prior knowledge will not be sufficient as it depends on the ZPD of students whether both prior knowledge and a help system (or a formal system) will add up to the appropriate learning outcomes. Whether a student is in a ZPD may depend on prior knowledge, intelligence, the ability to make (new) social or technical tools (e.g., resp. teachers and external representations) profitable, and motivation. At present, I do not know how to reconstruct this four-way interaction. Choosing first-year technical science students in chapter 7, was a reasonable interpolation as more advanced technical science students proved to be beyond the ZPD, while first-year social science students are not yet in it. However, such an empirical method is rather expensive and time-consuming and not very precise as only a group characteristic can be derived. ZPD should be measurable as a personal, though changeable attribute.

After finding a group result —as is usual in human reasoning research— based on hypotheses derived from a global theory, further progression should be attained by more specific research, directed towards individual processes (including the ZPD). A specific theory should be constructed within the developmental situativity framework concerning learning processes related to the resources and tasks within the instructional treatments. Greeno (personal communication, March 1995) suggests to use diagnostic test items as well as qualitative techniques like protocol analyses, conversations during collaborative thinking, and interviews for this purpose. Another type of specializing may be realized by computational construction in line with the computational theory as envisioned in the previous section. Empirical and computational results may be used to complement each other.

Although the near-transfer test has not proved to be very useful and it may not be very diagnostic for *specific* learning outcomes related to instructional differences, removal of the test may alter outcomes as it is unknown whether the test itself generates a learning effect[6] in combination with the SiD&F-instruction: The experiences during the test are still often counterintuitive (feedback is provided by Tarski's World during the test) and the subjects are highly aware of the test function of the items.

The precise functionality of the explanatory text also remains unclear. The unsuccessful manipulation in the first two experiments may have been

---

[6]In fact several subjects (of the experiment in chapter 7) believe they have learned during the tests: 50% of the SiD&F group, 6% of the SiD group, 17% of the F group, and 30% of the control group. Note that the control group only received the far-transfer test.

—partly— due to the absence of such a text, but comparison to the last experiment is not straightforward due to the instructional, technical, and methodological differences. In chapter 5, it was found that an explanatory text was as effective with as without instruction, except on the delayed PAC, where the text without further instruction was less productive than the text added with Tarski's World instruction. However, several arguments supported the post-hoc explanation that the sample was too experienced (i.e., beyond the ZPD for logical conditional reasoning). For these students, improvement appears to be related to a recognition of the appropriate fit between the situation and the material conditional, which was only moderately influenced by instructional interventions. An explanatory text did not facilitate logical reasoning in combination with only-formal or only-SiD instruction presented to less experienced students (see chapter 7), while it was effective in combination with SiD&F-instruction. These results support the assumption that an explanatory text functions as a catalyst or as an attention generator. However, as the last experiment was designed to estimate the effect of instruction, related to the effect of no instruction, no firm conclusion can be drawn to the effect of the explanatory text. Further research has to clarify the precise function and working of such text.

It is yet unclear whether SiD is guaranteed because students are merely working with Tarski's World in the context of the experiments (Duffy, personal communication, August 1994). There are two questions involved in this problem: (a) Is situativity-in-logic guaranteed?, and (b) Is transfer to a reasoning task outside the experimental environment possible? The first question should not be related to the authenticity of the task (see chapter 2), but the question is important. SiD is guaranteed when someone is able to act upon objects in a direct way, the processing and activity towards the object does not concern formal concepts, but everyday concepts. Meaning is not detached (into semantics) and reconstructed partially after a syntactic process, but it is an integral and even the central aspect of activity. The activity in the world window of Tarski's World is unproblematic (the use of the mouse and the arrow are hardly problematic even to inexperienced students), but the use of natural language is not always truly natural. Therefore, there is some uncertainty concerning the facilitating SiD potential of some natural expressions. The results of the last experiment prove that this problem is not severe.

I am less optimistic concerning the second question. In everyday life, most situations do not require fully abstract reasoning rules, and besides, applying them —logically correct— would often be wrong or irrelevant (see note 3). The everyday reasoning techniques, although sometimes erroneous, are often functional. Formal logic will not easily compete with everyday logic. It is not unlikely that successful Tarski's World students try to apply the modus tollens in some everyday life situation successfully, but for most conditional reasoning they will not rely on formal rules, and therefore, the rules will be extinct after a while. Formal logic, of course, has its powerful application in science and technology. In constructing technical applications or communicating about technical topics, a successful student will often apply the formal logic appropriately, which may lead to extinction of everyday reasoning in this particular environment. Regardless of the generalizability of the learning outcome, and whether such generalization would be desirable in all environments, the fact that logical conditional reasoning in far-transfer tasks could be facilitated after a short instruction is important in itself as it provides some insight into the nature of learning.

8.4 Instructional Implications

The developmental situativity theory may have a major impact on instructional science because it coherently combines the theory of situated cognition (the instructional view on situated action: Brown, Collins & Duguid, 1989) with constructivistic ideas (Jonassen, 1991), while it accords to a large extent with the computational learning theory of the Induction framework (Holland et al., 1986). In this section, I will explore the relevance of the developmental situativity theory for instructional theory and the kind of instructional design that may be based on it. I will do so by concentrating on logic instruction.[7]

The designer of an introduction to first-order logic should try to motivate all students, not only the ones who are attracted to the ivory tower atmosphere that logic still has. A small arcade-like environment may provide for several situations. Some of the situations may need everyday reasoning to survive, others may need a logical one. The student may have a (simulated) advisor who may suggest wrong or right decisions and who provides some reflection on the feedback. Such experiences are important to acknowledge the importance of logic without making everyday reasoning totally suspect and ridiculous. These

---

[7]Although Tarski's World can be seen as a good example of an instructional environment in line with the developmental situativity theory, the instructional treatment presented to subjects in this study is not considered to be an ideal example of an instructional application of the theory. The instructional treatment (SiD&F) only provided for a minimum of experiences to afford a competition between everyday conditional reasoning and the material conditional. The subjects did not gain a systematic overview of all logical connectives and they did not gain an understanding of the purpose of the connectives, the relations between them and the relations to their everyday pendants. This has not been the intention of this study, and consequently, when one is tempted to design a complete introduction to formal logic in line with the developmental situativity theory, one has to recognize that the exemplary role of the present experimental instruction is limited.

experiences may be referred to in order to explain the purpose of logic. The student should experience and understand that logic can be a powerful tool for some problems but that it is too strong for other problems (leading to irrelevant or wrong choices as it may abstract too much from everyday connotations). Logic may or may not be appropriate in everyday life situations, but it will be superior in technical and scientific environments: Logic is no more than a tool for tools.

These initial experiences and explanations will only require a couple of hours. When properly implemented it stimulates thinking and motivation, instead of crushing it. The student's attitude will be more directed to the use of logic than to its own failures. To understand that there is a difference between the 'logic' of everyday life and the logic of artifacts and that both systems have their own functionality and rationality (see chapter 3) will be a very relaxing idea before continuing the study of formal logic.

I do not imply that everyday reasoning is always superior in everyday life. For instance, the abstract Wason selection task is considered to be abstract because of the arbitrary relation between antecedent and consequent of the conditional, but in fact it is situated. The actual (or visually presented) cards and the rule in simple natural language constitute a situation with real-life properties, but one in which formal logic is evidently superior. As the task is situated, people will not easily apply the modus tollens even when they know the rule or when they understand explanation after a prior failure. Before applying the modus tollens, people will need considerable experience with formal systems during which they slowly develop the ability to recognize which situations afford the formal rule and which situations do not. In terms of the developmental situativity theory, the person's psychological reality has gained new affordances: Some situations appear to afford the modus tollens.

The use of Wason's selection task in this study is interesting for instructional science as it demonstrates the relevance of a simulated SiD-environment. Without simulation, feedback on situated action would not have been so consequently directed by formal logic. For that reason, all short-term instructional programs have failed to facilitate logical reasoning in the abstract Wason selection task except when used as a near-transfer task under certain conditions. However, the success of a simulated SiD-environment also evokes a new problem: The experiences with formal systems in a simulated SiD-environment may not be realistic and distorted. For instance, in the instructional treatment a formal system was applied to situations in which everyday reasoning appeared to be wrong, whereas in reality it would be correct. As the experiences can be strong, simulated SiD-environments may lead to a distorted concept of reality, especially when the student does not have the opportunity to experience the real SiD-environment. For conditional reasoning, this problem is not severe because there is hardly a day passing without some conditional reasoning in it. Therefore, the chance that formal reasoning will transfer for a long time to situations outside the experimental environment is low. Instructional simulations designers should avoid this problem by clarifying the purposes and the situations for which the formal system is constructed.

As logic instruction may not be prototypical due to its abstract subject, one may object that the conclusion —formal tools are needed during SiD— can be generalized to other domains. This critique seems reasonable as for many learning processes it is apparently sufficient only to act directly on the matter (situated learning) or to act merely by using formal symbols (formal education). Although these learning effects are not contradicted, they are considered to be uninteresting for educational purposes. Most learning processes in everyday life are situated, with concrete-symbolic, situative tools (everyday or basic-level concepts). Bereiter (1992) argues that it is not necessary to teach basic-level concepts as they are learned without much effort in everyday life. Instruction totally based on situated learning, therefore, is a waste of effort and time. Formal symbols (referring to abstract concepts), are useful as tools just because they lack situativity. Even without dual stimulation, some bright students may be able to play with formal systems quite handsomely —on near-transfer tasks— , without really knowing what they do and why they do it. For these students formal education seems successful, but what is likely to happen is that they learn to operate tools without understanding. As these students are bright, they may eventually understand the use of these tools in further education or in their jobs, but such a learning process is not efficient and it is ineffective for other students. Nevertheless, some students may be able to understand the use of the tool directly. In such cases instruction was inefficient too, as these students were already beyond the ZPD at the moment of instruction. Nearly any instruction would then be effective, but this is a fake effect as the student basically understood the concept or the method to be learned.

The implication of the developmental situativity theory for education is that formal systems should be presented as tools and not as objectives. These tools should be learned in everyday-like situations which attract attention to the usefulness of the tools. What is needed is insight in the type of problems in which formal concepts or systems may be used as tools. Education (at least secondary schools and beyond) should stimulate motivation (cf. Norman, 1994) to acquaint with these problems (problems should be situated, which is more than providing a concrete context in a textbook). Once students have profound insight in problems, they may be eager to solve them. Only then are students intrinsically motivated to learn about tools too.

Situated problems may be provided by authentic tasks, but also by computer based instruction in the form of interactive graphical representations of instances of everyday concepts and simulations of concrete matter, as for example in Tarski's World. A computer may not only substitute a physical environment but also a social environment (there may be agents for peers, supervisors, etc.) Computers may also be used to provide a personal instructional environment which is able to detect individual ZPD. Multimedia or virtual reality systems may be important for several domains, but most important condition for efficient and effective instruction is dual stimulation (formal tools in an environment that facilitates SiD) within the ZPD.

Another implication of the developmental situativity theory for education is the redundancy of the testing culture at schools. Instruction based on the developmental situativity theory has succeeded when a situated problem can be solved by using formal methods: The type of problems that can be solved by students simply indicates their level. Teachers do not have to spend time to construct and score tests which only measure knowledge about formal systems or restricted application of formal systems in non-situative problems.

Present instructional-design theories (for a slightly outdated but good overview, see Reigeluth, 1983) assume that formal concepts and systems can be transmitted to students via a formal description (following one method or another) in combination with presentation of examples, i.e., instances of concepts or a concrete context for formal systems (following one method or another). The acquisition of formal knowledge should in itself —due to its abstract nature— be sufficient to lead to transfer from the learning situation to another situation. As this has proved to be extremely difficult, more effort is put on the contexts (concrete, but not situated) in which formal systems can be applied: teaching for transfer. But again, transfer has not been found in research unless by the most generous criteria (Detterman, 1993).

From the developmental situativity perspective this is not surprising, because there are, as far as I know, no methods available to merge formal systems with SiD within each learning moment as is needed for far transfer. This thesis has pioneered on this topic theoretically as well as experimentally. For the development of such methods, it is suggested to combine elements out of instructional-design theories (especially methods to instruct formal systems; methods for contextualization may be less useful) with either elements out of cognitive apprenticeship or elements out of simulations research (as far as they concern interactive representations). This thesis has provided a constraint for a general instructional-design theory. Which elements and what combination of existing theories to choose will have to be the subject of future studies.

References

Agre, P.E. (1993). The symbolic worldview: Reply to Vera and Simon. *Cognitive Science, 17*(1), 61-70.

Anderson, J.R. (1983). *The architecture of cognition.* Cambridge, MA: Harvard University Press.

Anderson, J.R. (1990). *The adaptive character of thought.* Hillsdale, NJ: Lawrence Erlbaum Associates.

Anderson, J.R. (1992). *Cognitive psychology and its implications.* San Fransisco: W.H. Freeman and Company.

Anderson, L.W. (1981). Instruction and time-on-task: A review. *J. Curriculum Studies.* 13(4), 289-303.

Barwise, J. & Etchemendy, J. (1989). Model-theoretic semantics. In M.I. Posner (Ed.), *Foundations of cognitive science.* Cambridge, MA: The MIT Press, 207-243.

Barwise, J. & Etchemendy, J. (1990). *The language of first-order logic.* Stanford: Center for the Study of Language and Information.

Barwise, J. & Etchemendy, J. (1991). Visual information and valid reasoning. In W. Zimmermann & S. Cunningham (Eds.), *Visualization in teaching and learning mathematics*. Washington DC: Mathematical Association of America.

Barwise, J. & Etchemendy, J. (1995). *Hyperproof*. Stanford: Center for the Study of Language and Information.

Barwise, J. & Perry, J. (1983). *Situations and attitudes*. Cambridge, MA: The MIT Press.

Bereiter, C. (1991). Implications of connectionism for thinking about rules. *Educational Researcher, 20*(3), 10-16.

Bereiter, C. (1992). Referent-centred and problem-centred knowledge: Elements of an educational epistemology. *Interchange, 23*(4), 337-362.

Berry, D.C. (1983). Metacognitive experience and transfer of logical reasoning. *Quaterly Journal of Experimental Psychology, 35A*, 39-49.

Braine, M.D.S. (1978). On the relation between the natural logic of reasoning and standard logic. *Psychological Review, 85*, 1-21.

Braine, M.D.S. (1990). The "Natural Logic" approach to reasoning. In W.F. Overton (Ed.), *Reasoning, necessity, and logic: Developmental perspectives*, (pp. 135-158). Hilssdale, NJ: Lawrence Erlbaum Associates.

Braine, M.D.S., O'Brien, D.P. (1991). A theory of If: A lexica entry, reasoning program and pragmatic principles. *Psychological Review, 98*, 182-203.

Brooks, R.A. (1991a). Intelligence without representation. *Artifical Intelligence, 47*, 139-159.

Brooks, R.A. (1991b). How to built complex creatures rather than isolated cognitive simulators. In K. van Lehn (Ed.), *Architectures for Intelligence: The 22nd Carnegie Symposium on Cognition*. Hillsdale, NJ: Erlbaum.

Brown, J.S., Collins, A. & Duguid, P. (1989). Situated cognition and the culture of learning. *Educational Researcher, 17*, 32-41.

Cheng, P.W. & Holyoak, K.J. (1985). Pragmatic reasoning schemas. *Cognitive Psychology, 17*, 391-416.

Cheng, P.W., Holyoak, K.J., Nisbett, R.E. & Oliver, L.M. (1986). Pragmatic versus syntactic approaches to training deductive reasoning. *Cognitive Psychology, 18*, 293-328.

Clancey, W.J. (1991). Situated cognition: Stepping out of representational flatland. *AI Communications-The European Journal on Artificial Intelligence.* 4(1/2), 109-112.

Clancey, W.J. (1993). Situated action: A neuropsychological interpretation response to Vera and Simon. *Cognitive Science,* 17(1), 87-118.

Cosmides, L. (1989). The logic of social exchange: Has natural selection shaped how humans reason? Studies with the Wason selection task. *Cognition,* 31, 187-276.

Detterman, D.K. (1993). Case against transfer. In D.K. Detterman & R.J. Sternberg (Eds.), *Transfer on trial: Intelligence, cognition, and instruction* (pp. 1-24). Norwood, NJ: Ablex.

Duffy, T.M. & Jonassen D.H. (1992). Constructivism: New implications for instructional technology. In Duffy & Jonassen (Eds.), *Constructivism and the technology of instruction: A conversation* (pp. 1-16). Hillsdale, NJ: Lawrence Erlbaum Associates

Duffy, T.M., Lowyck, J. & Jonassen D.H. (1993). *Designing environments for constructivistic learning.* BerlIn Springer verlag.

Edelman, G.M. (1992). *Bright air, brilliant fire: On the matter of the mind.* New York: Basic books.

Evans, J.St B.T. (1982). *The psychology of deductive reasoning.* London: Routledge and Kegan Paul.

Evans, J.St.B.T. (1993). Bias and rationality. In K.I. Mankletow & D.E. Over (Eds.), *Rationality.* London: Routledge.

Evans, J.St.B.T., Newstead, S.E. & Byrne, R.M.J. (1993). *Human reasoning: The psychology of deduction.* Hove, UK: Lawrence Erlbaum Association.

Falmagne, R.J. (1975a). *Transfer on trial: Intelligence, cognition, and reasoning: representations and proces in children and adults.* Hillsdale, NJ: Lawrence Erlbaum Associates.

Falmagne, R.J. (1975b). Introduction. In R.J. Falmagne (Ed.), *Transfer on trial: Intelligence, cognition, and reasoning: representations and proces in children and adults.* Hillsdale, NJ: Lawrence Erlbaum Associates.

Falmagne, R.J. (1990). Language and the acquisition of logical knowledge. In W.F. Overton (Ed.), *Reasoning, necessity, and logic: Developmental perspectives* (pp. 111-134). Hillsdale, NJ: Lawrence Erlbaum Associates.

Fung, P., O'Shea, T., Bornat, R., Reeves, S. & Goldson, D. (1993). Fear of formal reasoning. *Proceedings of the World Conference on Artificial Intelligence in Education* (pp. 201-208). Edinburgh.

Gardner, H. (1985). *The mind's new science: A history of the cognitive revolution.* New York: Basic Books.

George, C. (1991). Facilitation in Wason's selection task with a consequent referring to an unsatisfactory outcome. *British Journal of Psychology, 82,* 463-472.

Gibson, J.J. (1966). *The senses considered as perceptual systems.* Boston: Houghton Mifflin.

Gibson J.J. (1986). *The ecological approach to visual perception.* Hillsdale, NJ: Lawrence Erlbaum Associates. (Original work published in 1979).

Gleitman, L.R., Armstrong, S.L. & Gleitman, H. (1983). On doubting the concept 'concept'. In E.K. Scholnick (Ed.), *New Trends in Conceptual Representation: Challenges to Piaget's Theory?* (pp. 87-110). Hillsdale, NJ: Lawrence Erlbaum Associates.

Goldson, D., Reeves, S. & Bornat, R. (1991). *A review of several programs for the teaching of Logic* (Tech. Rep.). London: University of London.

Goldson, D., Reeves, S. (1991). *"The Language of First Order Logic" including the Macintosh program "Tarski's World" - Jon Barwise and John Etchemendy Reviewed* (Techn. Rep. 546). London: University of London, Department of Computer Science.

Greeno, J.G. (1989). Situations, Mental Models, and Generative Knowledge. In D. Klahr & K.Kotovsky (Eds.), *Complex Information Processing: The impact of Herbert A. Simon,* (pp. 285-318). Hillsdale, NJ: Lawrence Erlbaum Associates.

Greeno, J.G. (1990). Productive learning envirinments. *Proceedings of the International Conference on Advanced Research on Computers in Education* (pp. 1-11). Tokyo, Japan.

Greeno, J.G. & Moore, J.L. (1993). Situativity and symbols: Response to Vera and Simon. *Cognitive Science, 17*(1), 49-60.

Greeno, J.G., Moore, J.L. & Smith, D.R. (1993). Transfer of situated learning. In D.K. Detterman & R.J. Sternberg (Eds.), *Transfer on trial: Intelligence, cognition, and instruction* (pp. 99-167). Norwood, NJ: Ablex.

Griggs, R.A. (1989). To "See" or not to "See": That is the selection task. *Quaterly Journal of Experimental Psychology, 41A,* 517-529.

Griggs, R.A. & Cox, J.R. (1982). The elusive thematic materials effect in the Wason's selection task. *British Journal of Psychology, 73,* 407-420.

Henle, M. (1962). On the relation beteen logic and thinking. *Psychological Review, 69,* 366-378.

Hodges, W. (1989). Review: "Tarski's World" and "Turing's World". *Computerised Logic Bulletin, 2*(1), 36-50.

Holland, J.H., Holyoak, K.J., Nisbett, R.E. & Thagard, P.R (1986). *Induction: Processes of inference, learning, and discovery.* Cambridge, MA: The MIT Press.

Holyoak, K.J. & Spellman, B.A. (1983). Thinking. *Annual Review of Psychology, 44,* 265-315.

Inhelder, B. & Piaget, J. (1958). *The growth of logical thinking.* New York: Basic Books.

Jonassen, D.H. (1991). Objectivism vs. constructivism: Do we need a new philosophical paradigm? *Educational Technology: Research & Development, 39*(3), 5-14.

Jonassen, D.H. (1992). Evaluating constructivistic learning. In T.M. Duffy & D.H. Jonassen (Eds.), *Constructivism and the technology of instruction: A conversation.* Hillsdale NJ: Lawrence Erlbaum Ass.

Johnson, M. (1987). *The body in the mind: The bodily basis of meaning, imagination, and reason.* Chicago: University of Chicago Press.

Johnson-Laird, P.N. (1983). *Mental models: Towards a cognitive science of language, inference, and conciousness.* Cambridge: Cambridge University Press.

Johnson-Laird, P.N., Herrmann, D.J. & Chaffin, R. (1984). Only connections: A critique of semantic networks. *Psychological Bulletin, 96*(2), 292-315.

Johnson-Laird, P.N., Legrenzi, P. & Legrenzi, M.S. (1972). Reasoning and a sense of reality. *British Journal of Psychology, 63,* 395-400.

Johnson-Laird, P.N. & Wason, P.C. (1970). A theoretical analysis of insight into a reasoning task. *Cognitive Psychology, 1,* 134-148.

Kirkby, K.N. (1994). Probabilities and utilities of fictional outcomes in Wason's four-card selection task. *Cognition, 51,* 1-28.

Lackoff, G. (1987). *Women, fire, and dangerous things: What categories reveal about the mind.* Chicago: The University of Chicago Press.

Lakatos, I. (1976). *Proofs and refutations: The logic of mathematical discovery.* Cambridge: Cambridge University Press.

Lave, J. (1988). *Cognition in practice: Mind, mathematics and culture in everyday life.* Cambridge: Cambridge University Press.

Lehman, D.R. & Nisbett, R.E. (1990). A longitudinal study of the effects of undergraduate training on reasoning. *Developmental Psychology, 26*(6), 952-960.

Mankletow, K.I. & Evans, J.St.B.T. (1979). Facilitation of reasoning by realism: Effect or non-effect? *British Journal of Psychology, 70,* 477-488.

Margolis, L. (1987). *Patterns, thinking and cognition: A theory of judgment.* Chicago, IL: University of Chicago Press.

Neisser, U. (1976). *Cognition and reality: Principles and implications of cognitive psychology.* San Francisco: W.H. Freeman.

Newell, A. & Simon, H.A. (1972). *Human problem solving.* Englewood Cliffs, NJ: Prentice-Hall.

Norman, D.A. (1986). Cognitive engineering. In D.A. Norman & S.W. Draper (Eds), *User centered sytem design: New perspectives in human-machine interaction* (pp. 31-61). Hillsdale, London: Lawrence Erlbaum Associates.

Norman, D.A. (1993). Cognition in the head and in the world: An introduction to the special issue on cognitive action. *Cognitive Science, 17*(1), 1-6.

Norman, D.A. (1994). Things that make us smart. In D.A. Norman (Ed.), *Defending human attributes in the age of the machine* (CD-ROM). New York: Voyager.

Osherson, D. (1975). Logic and models of logical thinking. In Falmagne, R.J. (Ed.), *Reasoning: Representation and proces in children and adults* (pp. 81-91). Hillsdale, NJ: Lawrence Erlbaum Associates.

Osherson, D. & Smith, E. (1981). On the adequacy of prototype theory as a theory of concepts. *Cognition, 9*(1), 35-58.

Pollard, P. & Evans, J.St.B.T. (1987). The influence between content and context effects in reasoning. *American Journal of Psychology, 100,* 41-60.

Posner, M.I. (1989). *Foundations of cognitive science.* Cambridge, MA: The MIT Press, 207-243.

Putnam, H. (1981). *Reason, truth, and history.* Cambridge: Cambridge University Press.

Quine, W.V. (1987). *Quiddities: An intermittently philosophical dictionary.* Cambridge, MA: The Belknap Press.

Quine, W.V. (1986). *Philosophy of logic.* 2nd edition. Cambridge, MA: Harvard University Press.

Raven, J.C. (1962). *Advanced progressive matrices: Sets I and II.* London: H.K. Lewis & Co.

Ravan, J.C, Court, J.H. & Raven, J. (1988). *Manual for Raven's progressive matrices and vocabulary scales. Section 4: Advanced progressive matrices sets I and II.* London: H.K. Lewis & Co.

Rips, L.J. (1989). The psychology of knights and knaves. *Cognition, 31,* 85-116.

Rosch, E. (1978). Principles of categorization. In E. Rosch & B.B. Lloyd (Eds.), *Cognition and categorization.* Hillsdale, N.J.: Lawrence Erlbaum Associates.

Rosch, E. (1983). Prototype classification and logical classification: The two systems. In E.K. Scholnick (Ed.), *New trends in conceptual representation: Challenges to Piaget's theory?* (pp. 73-86), Hillsdale, NJ: Lawrence Erlbaum Ass.

Rosch, E., Simpson, C. & Miller, R.S. (1976). Structural bases of typicality effects. *Journal of Experimental Psychology: Human Perception and Performance, 2,* 491-502.

Schneider, W. & Shiffrin, R.M. (1977). Controlled and automatic human processing: I. Detection, search, and attention. *Psychological Review, 84,* 1-66.

Staudenmayer, H (1975). Understanding conditional reasoning with meaningful propositions. In Falmagne, R.J. (Ed.), *Reasoning: representation and proces in children and adults* (pp. 55-80). Hillsdale, NJ: Lawrence Erlbaum Associates.

Suchman, L.A. (1987). *Plans and situated actions: The problem of human-machine communication.* Cambridge: Cambridge University Press.

Suppes, P. (1981). *University-level computer-assisted instruction at Stanford: 1968-1980.* Stanford, CA: Stanford University.

Thagard, P. (1989). Explanatory coherence. *Behavioral and Brain Sciences, 12,* 435-502.

Van Dalen, D. (1993). Constructivism in Mathematics. In C. van Dijkum & G. de Zeeuw (Eds.), *Methodological explorations in constructive realism* (pp. 6-29). Amsterdam: Sokrates Science Publisher.

Van der Pal, J. & Baars, G. (1994.). *Teaching first-order logic with Tarski's World: An interactive graphical representational system.* (Techn. rep. IST-MEMO-94-07), University of Twente, Enschede

Vera, A.H. & Simon, H.A. (1993). Situated action: A symbolic interpretation. *Cognitive Science, 17*(1), 7-48.

Vygotsky, L.S. (1978). *Mind in society: The development of higher psychological processes.* Cambridge, MA: Harvard University Press.

Vygotsky, L.S. (1987). Thinking and speech. In R. Rieber & A.S. Carton (Eds.), *The collected works of L.S. Vygotsky. Vol 1. Problems of general psychology.* New York: Plenum Press. (Original work published 1934)

Vygotsky, L.S. & Luria, A. (1994). Tool and symbol in child development. In R. van der Veer & J. Valsiner (Eds.), *The Vygotsky reader.* (pp. 99-174). Oxford: Blackwell.

Wallner, F. & Peschl, M. (1993). Cognitive science - an experiment in constructive realism; constructive realism - an experiment in cognitive science. In C. van Dijkum & G. de Zeeuw (Eds.), *Methodological explorations in constructive realism* (pp. 30-39). Amsterdam: Sokrates Science Publisher.

Wason, P.C. (1966). Reasoning. In B.M. Foss (Ed.), *New horizons in psychology.* Harmondsworth: Penguin.

Winograd, T. & Flores, F. (1987). *Understanding computers and cognition: A new foundation for design.* Reading, MA: Addison-Wesley.

Wittgenstein, L. (1992). *Filosofische onderzoekingen.* [Translation of Philosophical Investigations / Philosophische Untersuchungen. Oxford: Blackwell, 1953.] Meppel: Boom.

Yachanin, S.A. & Tweny, R.D. (1982). The effect of thematic content on cognitive strategies in the four-card selection task. *Bulletin of the Psychological Society, 19,* 87-90.

Samenvatting
(Dutch Summary)

Deze dissertatie doet verslag van onderzoek naar de werking van Tarski's World, computer-ondersteund onderwijs voor een introductie in mathematische logica. Met Tarski's World wordt de logica vanuit een semantisch perspectief benaderd, in tegenstelling tot andere computer-ondersteunde onderwijssystemen voor mathematische logica die zich direct richten op formele bewijsvoering. Gebruik van Tarski's World heeft onder meer tot doel dat studenten een formele taal goed leren hanteren. Elementair voor het correct gebruik van een logische taal is een goed begrip van de logische implicatie. Dat dit in de praktijk van logica-onderwijs moeilijk blijkt te zijn, illustreert een belangrijke bevinding uit de psychologie van deductief redeneren: Mensen maken van nature geen gebruik van een volledig abstracte redeneerstructuur voor voorwaardelijke uitdrukkingen. Leereffecten in abstract conditioneel redeneren zijn slechts in weinig studies gevonden, waarbij de effecten in een instructietechnologisch perspectief oninteressant of inefficiënt zijn. Tarski's World is dermate verschillend van ander logica-onderwijs en van instructiemateriaal in psychologisch redeneeronderzoek dat het alleen op grond hiervan al enig optimisme toelaat voor leren conditioneel redeneren. Daarnaast is er theoretische ondersteuning voor dergelijk optimisme.

Samenvatting (Dutch summary)

Tarski's World kan worden geïnterpreteerd als een omgeving met formele aspecten die niettemin gesitueerde-ontwikkelingstheoriegesitueerd handelen ('situated action') stimuleert door het gebruik van interactieve grafische representaties. In een situated action theorie staat symboolverwerking niet centraal. Handelen en denken vindt primair zonder cognitieve representaties plaats en kent daardoor niet de semantische problematiek van het cognitivisme. Betekenis is niet losgekoppeld van de werkelijkheid: mens en omgeving vormen te samen een psychologische werkelijkheid waarin handelen en denken volledig en inherent betekenisvol zijn. Volledig betekenisvol handelen en denken geeft slechts ruimte voor een beperkt functioneren. Voor tal van functies zijn echter abstracties nodig. Abstracties kunnen slechts als representaties worden gebruikt. De huidige psychologie van situated action is onduidelijk over de relatie tussen situated action en representaties. In deze dissertatie wordt een eerste poging gedaan om deze relatie te beschrijven met behulp van Vygotsky's ontwikkelingspsychologie. In de resulterende gesitueerde-ontwikkelingstheorie ('developmental situativity theory') wordt een evenwicht tussen gesitueerd handelen en formele instructie noodzakelijk geacht voor instructie om zowel effectief als efficient te kunnen zijn. In Tarski's World is een dergelijk evenwicht ingebouwd.

Het belang van het evenwicht tussen gesitueerd handelen en formele instructie wordt aangetoond door middel van onderzoek waarbij de effectiviteit van Tarski's World op conditioneel redeneren wordt vergeleken met de effectiviteit van twee versies van Tarski's World waarbij het evenwicht is verstoord: een versie die alleen gesitueerd handelen stimuleert en een versie die alleen formele instructie biedt. De gesitueerde-ontwikkelingstheorie wordt vergeleken met het inductie-raamwerk ('induction framework') van Holland, Holyoak, Nisbett & Thagard (1986). Beide theorieën erkennen het belang van ervaring (feedback op eigen handelen). Door ervaringen kan een reeds bestaande denkstructuur worden vervangen door een nieuwe denkstructuur. De twee instructies die gesitueerd handelen stimuleren, leiden tot dergelijke ervaringen waardoor de huidige denkstructuur voor conditioneel redeneren vervangen zou kunnen worden door een logische denkstructuur. Echter, de gesitueerde-ontwikkelingstheorie stelt dat de ervaringen slechts dan zinvol zijn als er symbolische middelen (een logische taal) beschikbaar zijn met behulp waarvan de betekenis van de oorspronkelijke denkstructuur losgekoppeld kan worden. De gesitueerde-ontwikkelingstheorie voorspelt alleen een leereffect in de volledige Tarski's World, terwijl het inductie-raamwerk leereffecten voorspelt in de condities die gesitueerd handelen stimuleren. Beide theorieën voorspellen ineffectiviteit van de instructie met alleen formele aspecten. De verwachting dat Tarski's World effectief is als gevolg van een combinatie van gesitueerd handelen en formele instructie staat centraal in het onderzoek.

Instructie tijdens de eerste twee experimenten (hofdstuk 5), met universitaire studenten, is uitsluitend gericht op ervaring. Er is geen tekst bijgevoegd over de materiële implicatie en de ervaringen worden niet nader toegelicht. Het leerproces wordt verondersteld volledig inductief te zijn. Hoewel technische en methodologische problemen tijdens deze eerste experimenten zodanig zijn dat er geen conclusie kan worden getrokken, is er geen plaats meer voor groot optimisme over de effectiviteit van Tarski's World. Ervaringen (met of zonder logische taal) blijken onvoldoende om een leereffect te bewerkstelligen.

In het derde experiment (hoofdstuk 6) ligt de nadruk op het effect van Tarski's World in interactie met uitleg. De instructie wordt versterkt met behulp van een tekst waarin een formele uitleg over de materiële implicatie en enkele concrete voorbeelden worden gegeven. Deze tekst wordt vooraf aan de proefpersonen aangeboden. Een tweede vorm van uitleg is het Spel, een interactieve formele bewijsvoering. Het experiment wordt uitgevoerd met drie condities: (a) Tarski's World met tekst, (b) Tarski's World met tekst en Spel, en (c) alleen tekst. De leereffecten voor alle condities zijn aanzienlijk en nauwelijks van elkaar verschillend afgezien van een positief na-effect voor de twee Tarski's World condities ten opzichte van de 'alleen tekst' conditie. Dat de instructie met alleen tekst toch een aanzienlijk leereffect oplevert is onverwacht voor de populatie proefpersonen die enige, maar toch beperkte ervaring heeft met formele systemen. Voorkennis blijkt een belangrijkere rol te spelen dan op grond van de literatuur en de eerste experimenten kon worden verwacht.

In het vierde en laatste experiment (hoofdstuk 7) wordt de hypothese achter de eerste twee experimenten opnieuw onderzocht. Er nemen proefpersonen deel met minder ervaring met formele systemen dan in experiment drie. De tekst met uitleg over de materiële implicatie wordt voorafgaand aan de Tarski's World condities (volledig, alleen gesitueerd handelen, alleen formele instructie) aangeboden. Een controlegroep krijgt geen instructie. De resultaten ondersteunen de hypothese duidelijk: Een combinatie van gesitueerd handelen en formele instructie is effectiever dan de andere twee instructievormen. De studenten die deze laatste instructievormen ontvingen hebben niet beter abstract leren redeneren dan de studenten in de controleconditie.

Geconcludeerd wordt dat de instructie in conditioneel redeneren slechts effectief en efficiënt is indien (a) gesitueerd handelen gestimuleerd wordt terwijl een formeel systeem gebruikt wordt als middel om de betekenis van voorwaardelijke uitspraken te wijzigen (of een nieuwe betekenisstructuur te maken), en (b) de instructie tijdig wordt aangeboden aan de geschikte doelgroep. Deze conclusie ondersteunt de gesitueerde-ontwikkelingstheorie en toont een tekortkoming van het inductie-raamwerk aan. Het voordeel van de laatste theorie is dat deze veel specifieker is over leerprocessen. De gesitueerde-ontwikkelingstheorie is hier onvolledig. Voor verdere theoretische ontwikkeling wordt voorgesteld diverse noties van het inductie-raamwerk om te zetten naar de gesitueerde-ontwikkelingstheorie.

Het onderzoek heeft geen duidelijkheid verschaft over het effect van de tekst over de materiële implicatie. Ook het belang van voorkennis is niet helder. Theoretisch wordt een verklaring gezocht in de 'zone of proximal development'. Empirisch is meer systematisch onderzoek nodig.

De implicaties voor de instructietheorie zijn veelvuldig. De gesitueerde-ontwikkelingstheorie als een synthese van 'situated cognition' en constructivisme geeft een nieuwe kijk op onderwijs die geheel anders is dan instructie die vanuit de afzonderlijke noties van 'situated cognition' of van constructivisme kan worden voorgesteld en die –paradoxaal genoeg– meer ruimte overlaat voor het gebruik van klassieke instructietheorieën.

Appendix A

Instructional Materials

A.1 Instructional Material for the Experiment of Chapter 7

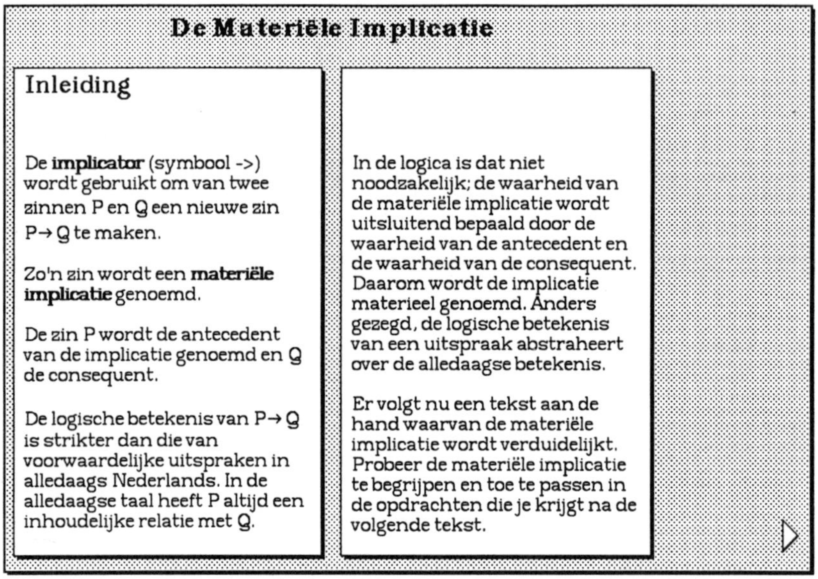

De Materiële Implicatie

Inleiding

De **implicator** (symbool ->) wordt gebruikt om van twee zinnen P en Q een nieuwe zin P→Q te maken.

Zo'n zin wordt een **materiële implicatie** genoemd.

De zin P wordt de antecedent van de implicatie genoemd en Q de consequent.

De logische betekenis van P→Q is strikter dan die van voorwaardelijke uitspraken in alledaags Nederlands. In de alledaagse taal heeft P altijd een inhoudelijke relatie met Q.

In de logica is dat niet noodzakelijk; de waarheid van de materiële implicatie wordt uitsluitend bepaald door de waarheid van de antecedent en de waarheid van de consequent. Daarom wordt de implicatie materieel genoemd. Anders gezegd, de logische betekenis van een uitspraak abstraheert over de alledaagse betekenis.

Er volgt nu een tekst aan de hand waarvan de materiële implicatie wordt verduidelijkt. Probeer de materiële implicatie te begrijpen en toe te passen in de opdrachten die je krijgt na de volgende tekst.

Figure A.1. Explanatory text about the material conditional: Introduction.

Translation of Figure A.1

Introduction. The symbol for the material conditional ($\rightarrow$) is used to combine two sentences P and Q to form a new sentence P $\rightarrow$ Q. Such a sentence is called a **material conditional**. The sentence P is called the antecedent of the conditional, and Q is called the consequent. The logical meaning of P $\rightarrow$ Q is more rigid than the meaning of conditionals in everyday Dutch. In natural language, P always has a sensible relation to Q. This is not necessary in logic. The truth value of a material conditional is determined only by the truth values of the antecedent and the consequent. This is why the conditional is called material. To put it differently: The logical meaning of a conditional is an abstraction of the natural meaning. A text follows which clarifies the material conditional. Try to understand the material conditional and try to apply it to the tasks that will be presented after the text.

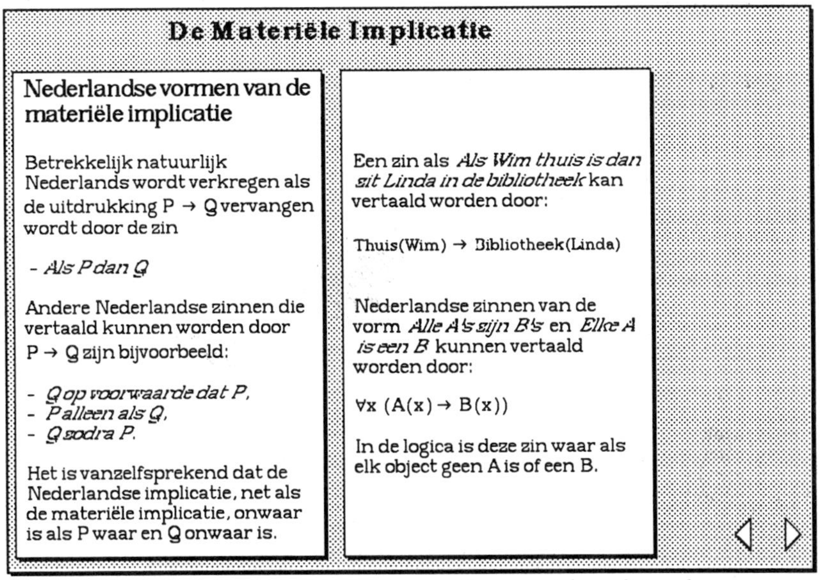

De Materiële Implicatie

Nederlandse vormen van de materiële implicatie

Betrekkelijk natuurlijk Nederlands wordt verkregen als de uitdrukking P → Q vervangen wordt door de zin

- *Als P dan Q*

Andere Nederlandse zinnen die vertaald kunnen worden door P → Q zijn bijvoorbeeld:

- *Q op voorwaarde dat P,*
- *P alleen als Q,*
- *Q zodra P.*

Het is vanzelfsprekend dat de Nederlandse implicatie, net als de materiële implicatie, onwaar is als P waar en Q onwaar is.

Een zin als *Als Wim thuis is dan zit Linda in de bibliotheek* kan vertaald worden door:

Thuis(Wim) → Bibliotheek(Linda)

Nederlandse zinnen van de vorm *Alle A's zijn B's* en *Elke A is een B* kunnen vertaald worden door:

∀x (A(x) → B(x))

In de logica is deze zin waar als elk object geen A is of een B.

Figure A.2. Explanatory text about the material conditional: Dutch forms of the material conditional.

Translation of Figure A.2

We can come fairly close to an adequate Dutch rendering of the expression P → Q with the sentence *If P then Q*. Other Dutch sentences that may be translated to P → Q are: *Q provided P, P only if Q*, and *Q when P*. At any rate, it is clear that Dutch conditionals, like the material conditional is false if P is true and Q is false. A sentence like *If Wim is at home than Linda is at the library* can be translated to: Home(Wim) → Library(Linda). Dutch expressions of the form *All A's are B's* and *Every A is a B* can be translated into: ∀x (A(x) → B(x)). In logic, this sentence is true when any object either fails to be an A or else be a B.

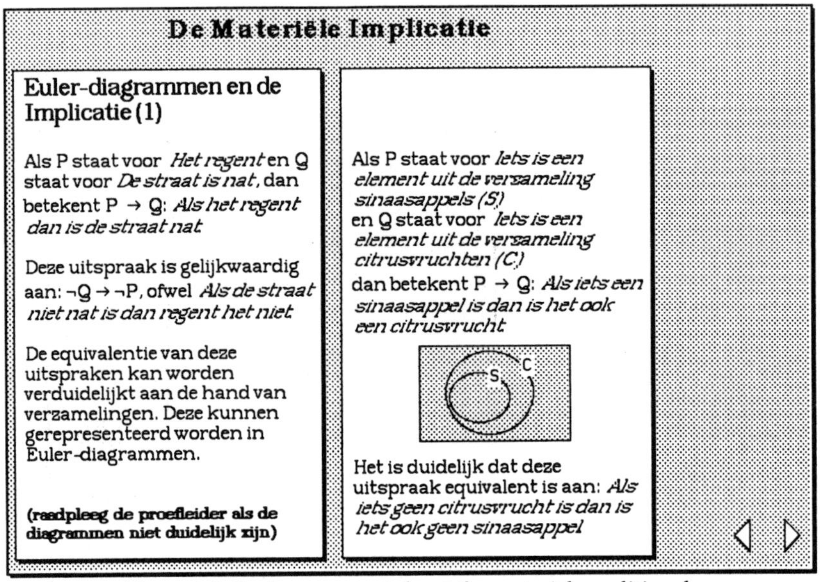

Appendix A

> ### De Materiële Implicatie
>
> **Euler-diagrammen en de Implicatie (1)**
>
> Als P staat voor *Het regent* en Q staat voor *De straat is nat*, dan betekent P → Q: *Als het regent dan is de straat nat*
>
> Deze uitspraak is gelijkwaardig aan: ¬Q → ¬P, ofwel *Als de straat niet nat is dan regent het niet*
>
> De equivalentie van deze uitspraken kan worden verduidelijkt aan de hand van verzamelingen. Deze kunnen gerepresenteerd worden in Euler-diagrammen.
>
> **(raadpleeg de proefleider als de diagrammen niet duidelijk zijn)**
>
> Als P staat voor *Iets is een element uit de verzameling sinaasappels (S)* en Q staat voor *Iets is een element uit de verzameling citrusvruchten (C)* dan betekent P → Q: *Als iets een sinaasappel is dan is het ook een citrusvrucht*
>
> Het is duidelijk dat deze uitspraak equivalent is aan: *Als iets geen citrusvrucht is dan is het ook geen sinaasappel*

Figure A.3. Explanatory text about the material conditional: Euler diagrams and the conditional (1).

Translation of Figure A.3:

Let P stand for *It is raining.* and let Q stand for *The pavement is wet*. Then P → Q says *If it is raining, then the pavement is wet*. This expression is equivalent to ¬Q → ¬P, saying *If the pavement is not wet, then it is not raining*. A way of understanding this equivalence is through the concept of sets. Sets can be represented by Euler diagrams. **(Consult the experimenter when the diagrams are not clear.)** Let P stand for *Something is an element in the set oranges (S).* and let Q stand for *Something is an element in the set citrus fruit (C).* Then P → Q means *If something is an orange, then it is also a citrus fruit.* It is evident that this statement is equivalent to *If something is not a citrus fruit, then it is not an orange either.*

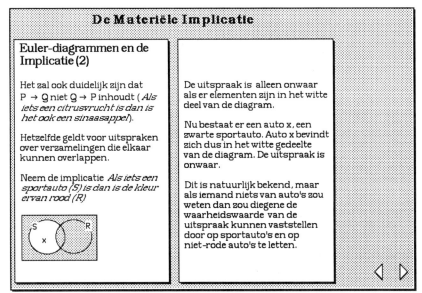

Figure A.4. Explanatory text about the material conditional:
Euler diagrams and the conditional (2).

Translation of Figure A.4

It will be equally evident that P → Q is not equivalent to Q → P (*If something is a citrus fruit, then it will also be an orange.*) This also holds for statements concerning overlapping sets. Consider the conditional *If something is a sportscar (S), then its color is red (R)*. This statement is only false when elements exists in the white part of the diagram. Now, a black sportscar x has been observed. Therefore, car x falls in the white part of the diagram. The conditional is false. Everybody knows this, but if someone would not know a thing about cars, then the truth value of the statement could be found by watching out for sportscars and for other than red cars.

Table A.1
Expressions used in the Instructional Treatment and their translations into English

Task	Expression	English Translation
A	1 Als a een tetraeder is dan is b een kubus.	If a is a tetrahedron then b is a cube.
	2 Als b een kubus is dan is a geen tetraeder.	If b is a cube then a is not a tetrahedron.
B	1 Als a een tetraeder is dan staat a voor d.	If a is a tetrahedron then a is in front of d.
	2 Als c klein is dan staat c rechts van a.	If c is small then c is to the right of a.
	3 Als a of c een tetraeder is dan is b of d een dodecaeder.	If a or c is a tetrahedron then b or d is a dodecahedron.
D	1 Alle dodecaeders zijn groot.	All dodecahedrons are large.
	2 Sommige dodecaeders zijn groot.	Some dodecahedrons are large.
	3 Als er een dodecaeder is dan zijn alle objecten groot.	If there is a dodecahedron then all objects are large.
	4 Er is iets waarvoor geldt dat als het een dodecaeder is, alle objecten groot zijn.	There is something for which holds that if it is a dodecahedron then all objects are large.
E	1 Elke middelgrote tetraeder staat voor b.	Each medium sized tetrahedron is in front of b.
	2 Elke kubus staat of voor b of achter a.	Each cube is in front of b or in back of a.
	3 Geen dodecaeder is klein.	No dodecahedron is small
F	1 Alle dodecaeders zijn kleiner dan alle kubussen.	All dodecahedrons are smaller than all cubes
	2 Alle objecten staan niet rechts van alle middelgrote kubussen.	All objects are not to the right of all medium sized cubes.
	3 Alle grote dodecaeders staan links van een kleine kubus.	All large dodecahedrons are to the left of a small cube.
G	1 Alle middelgrote objecten staan voor een object.	All medium sized objects are in front of an object.
	2 Alle objecten die voor een object staan zijn middelgroot.	All objects in front of an object are medium sized.
	3 Alle objecten die links van c staan zijn dodecaeders of ze zijn groot.	All objects to the left of c are dodecahedrons or large.

Note. Task C has not been used in any experiment reported in this thesis.

Instructional Materials 137

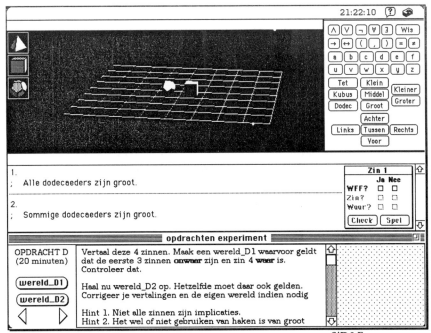

Figure A.5. The experimental environment for task D in the TW$^{\text{SiD\&F}}$ condition.

Table A.2

Example of (translated) task instructions and a possible solution to the task for each condition

Condition	Task D-instructions[a]	Possible solution[b]
TW$^{SiD\&F}$	Translate these 4 sentences. Construct a world_D1 in which the first 3 sentences are **false** and in which sentence 4 is **true**. Verify that. Then go to world_D2. The same must hold for this world. If needed, correct your translations and your own world. Hint 1. Not all sentences are conditionals. Hint 2. (Not) using parenthesis is crucial for sentences 3 and 4.	1. $\forall x\, (Dodec(x) \to Large\,(x))$ 2. $\exists x\, (Dodec(x) \land Large(x))$ 3. $\exists x\, Dodec(x) \to \forall y\, Large(y)$ 4. $\exists x\, (Dodec(x) \to \forall y\, Large(y))$ World_D1 contains 1 small dodecahedron and 1 small cube.
TW^{SiD}	Construct a world_D1 in which the first 3 sentences are **false** and in which sentence 4 is **true**. Verify that. Then go to world_D2. The same must hold for this world. If needed, correct your own world.	World_D1 contains 1 small dodecahedron and 1 small cube.
TW^{F}	Translate these 4 sentences. There is an invisible world in which the first 3 sentences are **false** and in which sentence 4 is **true**. Verify that. If needed, correct your translations. Hint 1. Not all sentences are conditionals. Hint 2. (Not) using parenthesis is crucial for sentences 3 and 4.	1. $\forall x\, (Dodec(x) \to Large\,(x))$ 2. $\exists x\, (Dodec(x) \land Large(x))$ 3. $\exists x\, Dodec(x) \to \forall y\, Large(y)$ 4. $\exists x\, (Dodec(x) \to \forall y\, Large(y))$

[a]see Table A.1, task D for the 4 sentences. [b]The possible solution for the world configuration is similar to world_D2.

Table A.3
Task-instructions of the near-transfer testitems and possible solutions

Test item	Task instruction	Possible solution
SiD&F	Sentence 1 is given: $\exists x \exists y (Large(x) \wedge Cube(x) \wedge Tet(y))$. World_WZ is given: a large cube and a small tetrahedron.	
	Translate sentence 2 ("There is an object for which holds that if it is large, there is a cube a and a dodecahedron b.")	$\exists x (Large(x) \rightarrow (Cube(a) \wedge Dodec(b))$
	Both sentences must be true in world_WZ. If needed, change the world and your translation, but **the world may contain at most 2 objects**. (meaning: change the two objects as you like, but do not add one).	A world with tetrahedron a and a large cube b.
F	Translate the sentence "All objects are small if there are no dodecahedrons." The expression must be true (in an invisible world). If needed, change your translation.	$\forall x \neg Dodec(x) \rightarrow \forall y\, Small(y)$
SiD	Verify the truth of the following natural sentences in world_W (in which a dodecahedron is left to a cube):	
	1. There is an object for which holds that if it is a cube, it stands to the left of a dodecahedron	1. true
	2. There is an object for which holds that if it is a dodecahedron, it stands to the left of a cube	2. true
	The translations are invisible. Assume that they are translated correctly (they are WFFs and Sentences). **Important:** Only verify once per sentence!	

Table A.4
Errortypes for the near-transfer test

Item	Errortype[a]	Counts as conditional error[b]
SiD&F	wrong use of predicates	+
	wrong connective	+
	severe syntax problems	-
	no parenthesis around expression	+
	wrong world configuration	+
	wrong quantifier	-
	using constants for variables vv	-
SiD	chosing false for sentence 1	+
	chosing false for sentence 2	+
F	switching antecedent - consequent	+
	wrong connective	+
	severe syntax problems	-
	wrong use of parenthesis	+
	wrong quantifier	-

[a] An item is solved correctly when it has none of the errors mentioned.
[b] Whenever an item contains conditional errors, it scores 1 point on the Conditional Errors variable.

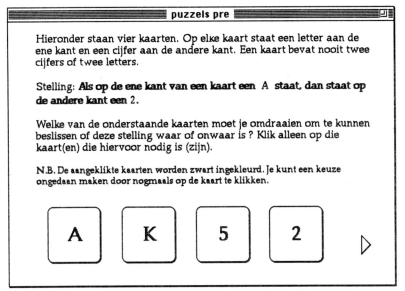

Figure A.6. The Wason selection task: Cards.

Translation of Figure A.6

Below are four cards. On each card a letter is printed on one side of the card and a number on the other side. A card never contains two numbers or two letters. Hypothesis: **If there is an A on one side of the card, there is a 2 on the other side.** Which of the cards below do you have to turn to decide whether the hypothesis is true or false? Click only on the card(s) that is (are) needed for your decision. Note. The clicked cards will become black. If you want to undo a choice, just click again on the card.

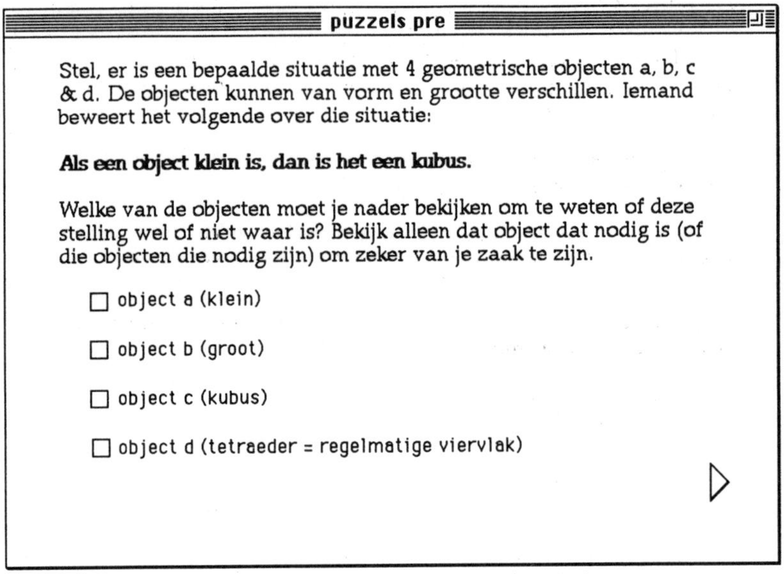

puzzels pre

Stel, er is een bepaalde situatie met 4 geometrische objecten a, b, c & d. De objecten kunnen van vorm en grootte verschillen. Iemand beweert het volgende over die situatie:

Als een object klein is, dan is het een kubus.

Welke van de objecten moet je nader bekijken om te weten of deze stelling wel of niet waar is? Bekijk alleen dat object dat nodig is (of die objecten die nodig zijn) om zeker van je zaak te zijn.

☐ object a (klein)

☐ object b (groot)

☐ object c (kubus)

☐ object d (tetraeder = regelmatige viervlak)

Figure A.7. The Wason selection task: Blocks.

Translation of Figure A.7

In a certain situation there are four geometric objects a, b, c , and d. The objects may differ in size and form. Someone makes the following assertion about the objects: **If an object is small, it is a cube.** Which of the following objects have to be examined to find out whether this assertion is true or not. Only observe that object or those objects necessary for your conclusion.

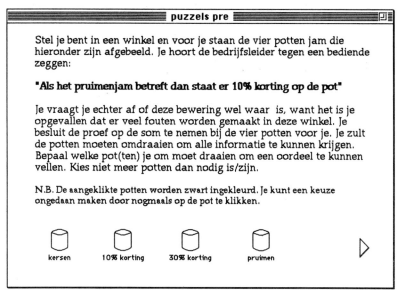

Figure A.8. The Wason selection task: Jars.

Translation of Figure A.8

Pretend you are in a shop and you see the four jars of jam that are shown below. At that moment you hear the manager saying to a salesclerk: **If it concerns plum jam, there is a 10% discount.** You wonder whether this is true because you experienced many mistakes in this shop. You decide to test the expression of the manager. Not all information can be read on one side of the jar, so you have to turn it around. Decide which jar(s) you have to turn to be able to test the expression. Do not chose more jars than necessary.

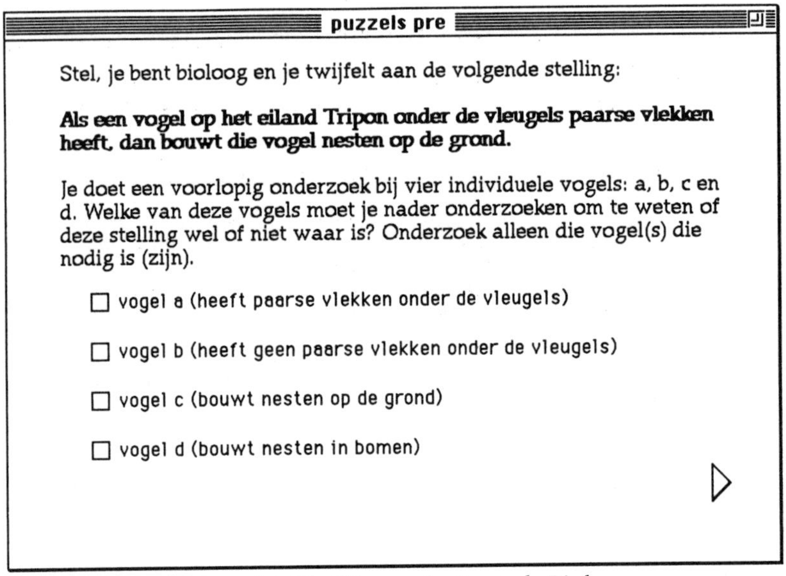

Appendix A

```
┌─────────────────── puzzels pre ───────────────────┐
│                                                   │
│   Stel, je bent bioloog en je twijfelt aan de volgende stelling: │
│                                                   │
│   **Als een vogel op het eiland Tripon onder de vleugels paarse vlekken │
│   heeft, dan bouwt die vogel nesten op de grond.** │
│                                                   │
│   Je doet een voorlopig onderzoek bij vier individuele vogels: a, b, c en │
│   d. Welke van deze vogels moet je nader onderzoeken om te weten of │
│   deze stelling wel of niet waar is? Onderzoek alleen die vogel(s) die │
│   nodig is (zijn).                                │
│                                                   │
│       ☐ vogel a (heeft paarse vlekken onder de vleugels) │
│                                                   │
│       ☐ vogel b (heeft geen paarse vlekken onder de vleugels) │
│                                                   │
│       ☐ vogel c (bouwt nesten op de grond)        │
│                                                   │
│       ☐ vogel d (bouwt nesten in bomen)           │
│                                                ▷  │
└───────────────────────────────────────────────────┘
```

Figure A.9. The Wason selection task: Birds.

Translation of Figure A.9

Pretend you are a biologist and you doubt the following hypothesis: **If a bird on the island Tripon has purple spots under its wings, it builds nests on the ground.** You conduct a pilot study with four individual birds: a, b, c, and d. Which of these birds do you have to examine more closely to find out whether the hypothesis is true or false? Only study that bird or those birds that are necessary for your conclusion.

A.2 Instructional Material for the Pilot Study of Chapter 5: Major Differences from the Material of Chapter 7

Table A.5
Expressions used in the instructional treatment for the pilot experiment of chapter 5 as far as they differ from Table A.1

Task	Expression	English Translation
B	4 Als b een kubus is, dan staat deze, mits b niet voor d staat, achter e.	If b is a cube, then it is to the back of e, provided that b is not in front of d.
	5 Als e geen tetraeder is dan is b of d klein.	If e is not a tetrahedron, then b or d is small.
D	3 Er is iets waarvoor geldt dat als het een dodecaeder is, groot is.	There is something for which holds that if it is a dodecahedron, it is large.
	4a	
E	4 Alle kubussen zijn klein.	All cubes are small.
F	3 Voor elke kubus en elke tetraeder geldt dat de ene links van de ander staat en andersom.	For each cube and for each tetrahedron holds that one is to the left of the other and the other way around.

Note. Task C has not been used in any experiment reported in this thesis. These sentences, combined with the sentences of Table A.1 form the 20 basic sentences for the three conditions of the pilot experiment.
[a]Sentence 4 of task D is not yet included.

Table A.6

Example of (translated) task instructions and a possible solution to the task for each condition

Condition	Task D-instructions[a]	Possible solution[b]
TW^{SiD&F}	Translate these 3 sentences. Construct a world_D1 in which the first 2 sentences are **false** and in which sentence 3 is **true**. Verify that. Then go to world_D2. The same must hold for this world. If needed, correct your translations and your own world.	1. $\forall x\,(Dodec(x) \rightarrow Large\,(x))$ 2. $\exists x\,(Dodec(x) \wedge Large(x))$ 3. $\exists x\,(Dodec(x) \rightarrow Large(x))$ World_D1 contains 1 small dodecahedron and 1 small cube.
TW^{SiD}	Construct a world_D1 in which the first 2 sentences are **false** and in which sentence 3 is **true**. Verify that. Then go to world_D2. The same must hold for this world. If needed, correct your own world.	World_D1 contains 1 small dodecahedron and 1 small cube.
TW^F	Translate these 3 sentences. There is an invisible world in which the first 2 sentences are **false** and in which sentence 3 is **true**. Verify that. If needed, correct your translations.	1. $\forall x\,(Dodec(x) \rightarrow Large\,(x))$ 2. $\exists x\,(Dodec(x) \wedge Large(x))$ 3. $\exists x\,(Dodec(x) \rightarrow Large(x))$

[a] see Tables A1 and A.5, task D for the 3 natural sentences. [b] The possible solution for the world configuration is similar to world_D2.

A.3 Instructional material for the Experiment of Chapter 5: Major Differences from the Material of Chapter 7

Table A.7
Expressions used in the instructional treatment for the experiment of chapter 5 as far as they differ from Table A.1

Task	Expression	English Translation
B	4 Als b een kubus is, dan staat deze, mits b niet voor d staat, achter e.	If b is a cube, then it is to the back of e, provided that b is not in front of d.
	5 Als e geen tetraeder is dan is b of d klein.	If e is not a tetrahedron, then b or d is small.
D	3 Er is iets waarvoor geldt dat als het een dodecaeder is, groot is. 4a	There is something for which holds that if it is a dodecahedron, it is large.
F	3 Voor elke kubus en elke tetraeder geldt dat de ene links van de ander staat en andersom.	It says that for each cube and for each tetrahedron, one is to the left of the other and the other way around.

[a]Sentence 4 of task D is not yet included.

A.4 Instructional material for the Experiment of Chapter 6: Major Differences from the Material of Chapter 7

Translation of Figure A.10

Terminology. The symbol for the material conditional ($\rightarrow$) is used to combine two sentences P and Q to form a new sentence P $\rightarrow$ Q. Such a sentence is called a **material conditional**. The sentence P is called the antecedent of the conditional, and Q is called the consequent. In this text, the logical meaning of the conditional will be described along with several Dutch examples. **Read carefully.**
Semantics of the conditional. The sentence P $\rightarrow$ Q is only true if P is true or Q is false. Therefore, P $\rightarrow$ Q is another expression for $\neg$P $\vee$ Q.

Truth table:

P	Q	P $\rightarrow$ Q
true	true	true
true	false	false
false	true	true
false	false	true

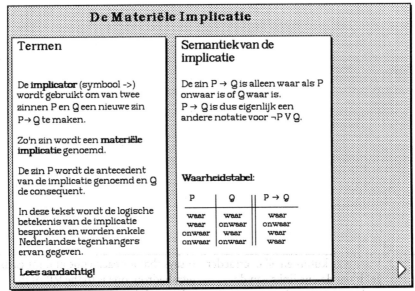

Figure A.10. Explanatory text about the material conditional: Terminology and Semantics of the material conditional.

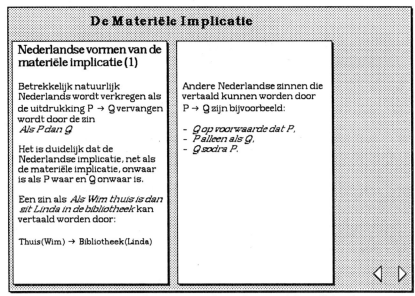

Figure A.11. Explanatory text about the material conditional:
Dutch forms of the material conditional (1).

Translation of Figure A.11

We can come fairly close to an adequate Dutch rendering of the expression P → Q with the sentence *If P then Q*. It is evident that Dutch conditionals, like the material conditional is false if P is true and Q is false. A sentence like *If Wim is at home than Linda is at the library* can be translated into: Home(Wim) → Library(Linda). Other Dutch sentences that may be translated into P → Q are: *Q provided P, P only if Q*, and *Q when P*.

De Materiële Implicatie

Nederlandse vormen van de materiële implicatie (2)

Het belangrijkste gebruik van → is in samenhang met de universele quantor (∀).

Nederlandse zinnen van de vorm *Alle A's zijn B's* en *Elke A is een B* kunnen vertaald worden door:

∀x (A(x) → B(x))

Als deze zin waar is, zal elk object óf geen A zijn óf een B zijn.

Niet elke Nederlandse *Als ... dan ...* kan door → vertaald worden.

Bijvoorbeeld:

De zin *Als Linda aan het werk geweest zou zijn dan zou Wim ook aan het werk geweest zijn* is onwaar als Linda bijvoorbeeld ziek was. Dit betekent dat de zin onwaar kan zijn als Linda niet aan het werk was. De waarheid van een zin als deze hangt dus niet alleen af van de waarheid van de delen.
De eerste orde zin

Werk(Linda) → Werk(Wim)

is daarentegen altijd waar als Linda niet aan het werk was!

In de opdrachten en toetsen krijgt u te maken met goed te vertalen Nederlandse zinnen.

Figure A.12. Explanatory text about the material conditional: Dutch forms of the material conditional (2).

Translation of Figure A.12

Most important use of → is in relation to the universal quantifier (∀). Dutch expressions of the form *All A's are B's* and *Every A is a B* can be translated into: ∀x (A(x) → B(x)). If this sentence is true then any object either fails to be an A or else be a B. Not every Dutch *If ... then ...* can be translated by →. For example: The sentence *If Linda had been at work, then Wim would also have been at work.* can be false for instance when Linda was ill. The truth of a whole sentence like this not only depends on the truth of its parts. In contrast, the first-order sentence Work(Linda) → Work(Wim) is always true when Linda was not working! Note that during the tasks and the tests you will work with Dutch sentences that can be translated to first-order logic adequately.

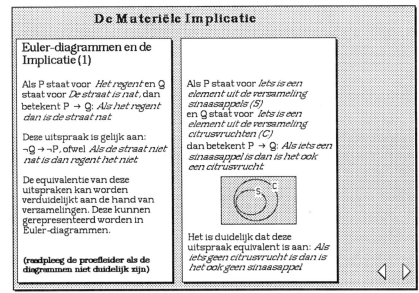

Figure A.13. Explanatory text about the material conditional:
Euler diagrams and the conditional (1).

Translation of Figure A.13

Let P stand for *It is raining.* and let Q stand for *The pavement is wet*. Then P → Q says *If it is raining, then the pavement is wet*. This expression is equivalent to ¬Q → ¬P, saying *If the pavement is not wet, then it is not raining*. A way of understanding this equivalence is through the concept of sets. Sets can be represented by Euler diagrams. **(Consult the experimenter when the diagrams are not clear.)** Let P stand for *Something is an element in the set oranges (S).* and let Q stand for *Something is an element in the set citrus fruit (C).* Then P → Q means *If something is an orange, then it is also a citrus fruit.* It is evident that this statement is equivalent to *If something is not a citrus fruit, then it not an orange either.*

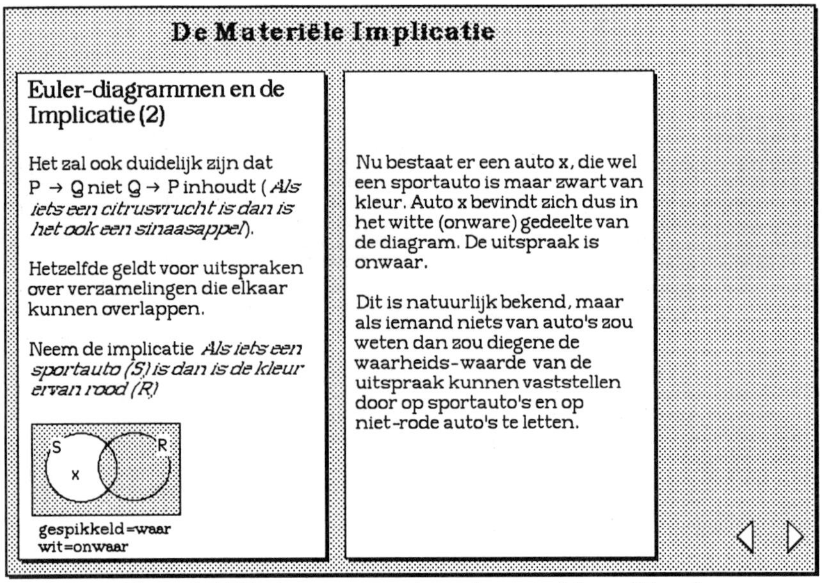

Figure A.14. Explanatory text about the material conditional:
Euler diagrams and the conditional (2).

Translation of Figure A.14

It will be equally evident that P → Q is not equivalent to Q → P (*If something is a citrus fruit, then it will also be an orange.*) This also holds for statements concerning overlapping sets. Consider the conditional *If something is a sportscar (S), then its color is red (R)*. Now, a black sportscar x has been observed. Therefore, car x falls in the white part of the diagram. The conditional is false. Everybody knows this, but if someone would not know a thing about cars, then the truth value of the statement could be found by watching out for sportscars and for other than red cars.

Table A.8

Expressions used in the Instructional Treatment for the experiment of chapter 6 as far as they differ to Table A.1

Task	Expression	English Translation
D	3 Er is iets waarvoor geldt dat als het een dodecaeder is, groot is. 4[a]	There is something for which holds that if it is a dodecahedron, it is large.
F	3 Voor elke kubus en elke tetraeder geldt dat de ene links van de ander staat en andersom.	For each cube and for each tetrahedron, the one is to the left of the other and the other way around.

[a]Sentence 4 of task D is not yet included.